Mark My Words

Mark My Words

Profiles of Punctuation in Modern Literature

Lee Clark Mitchell

BLOOMSBURY ACADEMIC
NEW YORK • LONDON • OXFORD • NEW DELHI • SYDNEY

BLOOMSBURY ACADEMIC
Bloomsbury Publishing Inc
1385 Broadway, New York, NY 10018, USA
50 Bedford Square, London, WC1B 3DP, UK

BLOOMSBURY, BLOOMSBURY ACADEMIC and the Diana logo are trademarks of
Bloomsbury Publishing Plc

First published in the United States of America 2020

Cover image: Jason Anscomb / rawshock design

Library of Congress Cataloging-in-Publication Data
Names: Mitchell, Lee Clark, 1947- author.
Title: Mark my words: profiles of punctuation in modern literature /
Lee Clark Mitchell.
Description: New York: Bloomsbury Academic, 2020. | Includes
bibliographical references and index. | Summary: "Shows how punctuation
and personality are intertwined through profiles of classic modernist
authors"– Provided by publisher.
Identifiers: LCCN 2019045408 | ISBN 9781501360732 (hardback) |
ISBN 9781501360749 (epub) | ISBN 9781501360756 (pdf)
Subjects: LCSH: English language–Punctuation. | Punctuation. |
Punctuation–Philosophy. | Punctuation–In literature.
Classification: LCC PE1450 .M58 2020 | DDC 421/.1–dc23
LC record available at https://lccn.loc.gov/2019045408

ISBN: HB: 978-1-5013-6073-2
PB: 978-1-5013-6072-5
ePDF: 978-1-5013-6075-6
eBook: 978-1-5013-6074-9

Typeset by Deanta Global Publishing Services, Chennai, India
Printed and bound in the United States of America

To find out more about our authors and books visit www.bloomsbury.com and sign
up for our newsletters.

What a hazard an Accent is! When I think of the
Hearts it has scuttled or sunk, I almost fear to lift my
Hand to so much as a punctuation.

> *Penciled draft (summer 1885) found among Emily*
> *Dickinson's papers (Dickinson, Letters 3: 887)*

The writer is in a permanent predicament when it comes to
punctuation marks; if one were fully aware while writing,
one would sense the impossibility of ever using a mark of
punctuation correctly and would give up writing.

> *Theodor Adorno (1956) (Adorno 305)*

The pace at which this world unfolds is supervised
by punctuation.

> *Fredric Jameson (1961) (Jameson, Sartre 41)*

The ear does it. The ear is the only true writer and the only true
reader. I have known people who could read without hearing the
sentence sounds and they were the fastest readers. Eye readers
we call them. They can get the meaning by glances. But they
are bad readers because they miss the best part of what a good
writer puts into his work.

   Remember that the sentence sound often says more than the
words. It may even as in irony convey a meaning opposite to
the words.

> *Robert Frost, letter to John Bartlett,*
> *February 22, 1914 (Frost 176)*

A woman without her man is nothing.
A woman: without her, man is nothing.

For Cameron, again

A woman: without her . . .

Contents

Acknowledgments

This book started as a slightly whimsical paper for a Santa Fe conference on "Sights and Sites: Vision and Place in American Literature," where I opened with a hypothetical:

> What if one stepped back from the echoing homonyms of this conference—physical sites and ocular sights (or rather, geographical places and symbolic visions)—to consider a map more familiar to most of us: the authorial landscape itself? And rather than gaze outward at cliffs, creeks, and crossroads, why not turn an eye instead to the topographies of punctuation that signal a writer's signature style?

The paper went well enough, but once I had returned home the questions it raised continued to grip me and wouldn't let go. And I in turn badgered various friends, only to be met by an outpouring of sprightly ripostes and recommendations, surprising me with the enthusiasm shared for a subject that generally flies under the radar. After all, who would suppose that punctuation could be a conversation stopper?

As it happened, many others have been fascinated by the squiggly marks shaping the words we read. And in the course of writing this monograph, I have benefited greatly from their acumen. Dan Fischer alerted me to W. G. Sebald's silencing dashes as well as José Saramago's uncorseted syntax; Maria DiBattista recommended Gertrude Stein (as Mona Zhang had, memorably, years before); Brian Gingrich reminded me of Laurence Sterne and Gustave Flaubert; Jim Longenbach rightly turned me back to poetry; and Garrett Stewart plumped for Cormac McCarthy, Max Beerbohm, Toni Morrison, and even more James. Each of these four also graciously, generously, put aside their own work to read an earlier version of the manuscript, offering unwanted advice (always useful), irritating corrections (ever accepted), and wonderfully suggestive ideas for shaping the whole (on which I've readily drawn). At Bloomsbury, Haaris Naqvi proved again a supportive editor whose enthusiasm and better sense for what a book should be forced me back to revisions. Most of all Cameron Platt was there at the beginning with challenging readings, better phrasings, even suasive punctuation. This book, as the dedication declares, was written first and above all for her, in playful celebration of an intellectual partnership that inspires, and a love that astonishes. The only way to describe the feeling is as a sequence of ever-sustaining semicolons and tumbling exclamation points . . . though you'll have to read on to see what I mean.

Permissions

Prologue: What Can Punctuation Do?

Maneuvering through unsettled landscapes of literary expression demands the occasional guard rails and blinking lights of punctuation: the jersey dividers and cautioning signs that serve as typographical tools for modifying syntax. Creativity needs constraints—and flourishes within them—requiring that unruly strings of words be policed into governable shape, transforming potential conflicts into the plausible constructions we intend (hence the crucial comma in "let's eat, grandma").[1] The fear that syntax alone may not be enough led Theodor Adorno to revere punctuation, even to the extent of lionizing the "definitive

---

[1]For a wry example of the dire semantic effects of punctuation, compare two versions of this heartfelt "Dear John" letter:

Dear John,

I want a man who knows what love is all about. You are generous, kind, thoughtful. People who are not like you admit to being useless and inferior. You have ruined me for other men. I yearn for you. I have no feelings whatsoever when we're apart. I can be forever happy—will you let me be yours?

Jane

Dear John,

I want a man who knows what love is. All about you are generous, kind, thoughtful people, who are not like you. Admit to being useless and inferior. You have ruined me. For other men, I yearn. For you, I have no feelings whatsoever. When we're apart, I can be forever happy. Will you let me be?

Yours,

Jane (https://www.vappingo.com/word-blog/the-importance-of-punctuation/)

physiognomic status" of every separate mark, each colorfully displayed: "All of them are traffic signals . . . Exclamation points are red, colons green, dashes call a halt" (Adorno 300).[2] Mary Oliver has further speculated in a parsimonious spirit that writers are each granted only "a finite amount of it for our use, and we should use it judiciously—lest we hear a voice, suddenly, when we need, saying, 'No more semicolons! You're finished with your dashes!'—and, also, that passive-aggressive comma, with which we so carefully set off what is nice, so it won't be missed" (Oliver). For Oliver, punctuation clamors to be invoked circumspectly, though her proof at last was to offer a poem shorn of any punctuation at all. And Adorno would have agreed, having already observed of his own acute "ascetic use": "In every punctuation mark thoughtfully avoided, writing pays homage to the sound it suppresses" (Adorno 305).

Still, poet and critic remain at odds over whether punctuation clarifies meaning or merely reaffirms what syntax already enacts, with clauses in proper order, depending on marks solely for stress. In either case, it might be better to think of punctuation less as regulation (like Adorno's imagined traffic stop, where speeding and prohibited turns are rigidly patrolled) than as a choice among distinct rhetorical effects, say commas rather than periods, or even more intriguingly rather than dashes. Keep in mind that

---

[2]Interestingly, the German word here is *Verkehrssignale*, and *Verkehr* means both traffic and communication. Moreover, as Adorno opened his celebrated 1956 essay: "The less punctuation marks, taken in isolation, convey meaning or expression and the more they constitute the opposite pole in language to names, the more each of them acquires a definitive physiognomic status of its own, an expression of its own, which cannot be separated from its syntactic function but is by no means exhausted by it." He then with a whimsical turn observed: "An exclamation point looks like an index finger raised in warning; a question mark looks like a flashing light or the blink of an eye. A colon, says Karl Kraus, opens its mouth wide: woe to the writer who does not fill it with something nourishing. Visually, the semicolon looks like a drooping moustache; I am even more aware of its gamey taste. With self-satisfied peasant cunning, German quotation marks (<< >>) lick their lips" (Adorno 300).

punctuation is exclusive to written texts, first appearing only after writing had been well-established. As John Lennard observes, "The earliest unit of punctuation in the West was the paragraph, which dates from the second century BC; but for nearly a millennium the paragraph had no internal punctuation other than that supplied by readers" (Lennard 2). If punctuation is not essential to sorting out verbal meaning, then, the question that remains is how it does or (more interestingly) does not imitate the effect of spoken stresses and pauses. What happens when we no longer consider it simply a marker for rhythms of speech?

That way of regarding the issue has enjoyed a centuries-long history, ever since the Roman Catholic Church introduced forms of punctuation (those, at least, more fine-tuned than paragraphing) to assist clerics in scriptural readings aloud. By the time Maggie Tulliver scolds her brother Tom in George Eliot's *The Mill on the Floss* (1860), the role of idiosyncratic marks as guide for public speaking had long been firmly entrenched, if only as an assist to breath control: "you don't mind your stops. You ought to stop twice as long at a semicolon as you do at a comma, and you make the longest stops where there ought to be no stops at all" (Eliot 140). Yet early on, the Church had realized the problem was not simply a matter of catching one's breath but of reinforcing liturgical control, in the escalating need to affirm orthodox meanings and otherwise rein in dissident ecclesiastical possibilities.[3] That bifurcated history helps explain modern linguists' own division, in the clash between a history of punctuation as largely oral development and more contemporary understandings of it as semantic discrimination.[4]

---

[3]On "the desire of the Catholic Church to prevent heterodoxy and heresy," see Lennard (2). As Jonathan Rée adds: "One plausible theory about punctuation marks is that they are originally and essentially guides to reading aloud; and people reading from a script may be accused of outright mistakes if they fail to obey the instructions supposedly implied by its punctuation" (Rée 1041).

[4]Among more important scholars of the early shift from orality to literacy was Walter Ong, who declared of "punctuation marks which the early grammarians

Intriguingly, this divergence launches striking questions for writers of both poetry and prose, especially given the incompatible pressures of different mediums: Why are Emily Dickinson and Henry James drawn habitually to the abrupt, protracted stretch of a dash? Why does James Baldwin relish Oliver's "passive-aggressive" commas while William Carlos Williams so assiduously avoids them? And why do both the novelist Virginia Woolf and the short-story specialist Andre Dubus II—surely an odd transatlantic pairing—eagerly embrace the ever-hesitant semicolon? More importantly, what suasive effect do such marks have on any characteristic perspective, certainly one that appears distinctively *authored* in all its swerves and delays?

The following discussion promises nothing like an exhaustive analysis, though it surveys familiar writers to inquire into their shapings of syntax, teasing out in the contrast among them the larger implications of what seem like arbitrary preferences for differing forms of punctuation. How, I ask, do nonverbal marks of celebrated writers' prose reveal at once characteristic styles and encompassing visions? More particularly, how do distinctions between punctuation and syntax help clarify what so often goes unnoticed, with some writers acceding to word order (embracing punctuation that seems nearly invisible) and others requiring sharp deflections (making us wonder at weird verbal rhythms). What, in short, is the difference between Willa Cather, whose syntax ordains her punctuation, and William Faulkner, who flagrantly ignores grammar with punctuation that works only rhetorically?

First, however, consider those who tend to ask such questions. With a few salient exceptions, punctuation has been a subject

mention, the clarification of the syntax is coincidental. The grammarians are interested primarily in the exigencies of breathing. It is convenient to place the breath pauses, and consequently the punctuation marks, where they will not interfere with the sense. But interest in both breathing and sense is quite independent of formal attention to grammatical structure" (Ong 351). See as well M. B. Parkes (esp. 11, 41) and Jeff Scheible (10).

left to buttoned-down grammarians and middle-school teach-
ers, who regularly censure us for breaking presumptive rules.[5]
Eric Partridge was hardly the first in 1953 to officiously set up
shop parceling out advice on ways typographical marks ease verbal expression (in the process deftly surveying three centuries of
such conventional wisdom). Yet he acknowledged the shifting
give-and-take involved in any such rules, conceding that "One
could write a monograph upon the psychological principles of
punctuation," though he himself demurred from taking up the
challenge (Partridge 7). Three decades later, Charles F. Meyer
opined (with a more fervent logic) that separation and enclosure
formed the basic premises of punctuation (Meyer). And standard
grade-school primers ever since have confirmed a vision of prose
as words herded into subordinate clauses, then clauses diverted
in turn.

The following discussion parts ways with conventional understanding by favoring writers who flagrantly break the rules.
They punctuate less as prod to drive preconceived meanings into
syntactical chutes, or otherwise as gentle nudge to avoid un-
sought impropriety, than as something of an alternative narrative universe that displaces the primacy of meaning by presenting
the reader with either disquieting disorder or unexpected ease.
Instead of a highway along which traffic signals facilitate well-
routed significance, we are presented with a theme-park ride of
careens, lurches, and glides. And rather than sense preceding
punctuation, with syntax dictating understanding, prose semantics emerge as the decided effects of what might seem like diacritical marks (marks that commonly have to do with a letter, not
a word). The work of punctuation can indeed encroach on meaning *as if from within*, with a dash or parenthesis, for instance, becoming almost a diacritical inflection of what it anticipates. No

---

[5]Two standard recent examples are Mignon Fogarty and M. B. Parkes. For an earlier
instance, see F. Horace Teall, as well as Gertrude Stein's famously idiosyncratic
personal essay. Lynn Truss offers a recent playful effort, but see Louis Menand's
critique.

longer are prior, purely verbal depictions parsed by the apparatus of typographical marks well after the fact; instead, marks dictate the message, making words seem momentarily secondary, teetering us initially on the edge of an Oxford comma, hesitating at a shy semicolon, reversing course with a swung dash, or unexpectedly sliding down slippery inclines without our having been exhorted to pause before the diction we traverse.[6]

In this roller-coaster domain, the demands of interruption, of swift swerves and abrupt full stops, become more important than whatever literal significance is demanded as the focus of our attention. Local rhetorical rhythms come to matter more than blanketing paraphrase; syncopation trumps sense as a series of sideslipping, lurching clauses waylay us from their ostensible claims of reference. Often as not, disruptions in reading become the essential meaning itself, even as those disruptions (involving deliberately missed punctuation, or alternatively an apparently unneeded mark) offer a vanishing point in which we are forced to pause. As John Lennard alleges of any punctuation, gathering it all under the rubric of "parenthesis": "The relationship between a parenthesis and its context is exactly a contrast between an absolute meaning, typographically isolated, and a relative meaning, typographically interposed. It is that double quality of the parenthetical" that lies at the heart of any and all interpretive gestures (Lennard 212).[7] And that "double quality" can surprise us as we see how a hiatus here, a dovetailed transition there, a lapidary gap or emotive lapse in a further text, can be systemized in something

---

[6]Dramatic proof that punctuation has crucial legal implications is the 2014 suit brought by three Maine truck drivers against Oakhurst Dairy for what they said was four years' worth of denied overtime pay. The case, which hung on a missing serial (or Oxford) comma, was settled for five million dollars. See Daniel Victor.

[7]For Lennard, views of punctuation split along party lines, with "the grammarians' insistence that parentheses are additional, irrelevant, extraneous, subordinate, or damaging to the clarity of argument: whereas in practice they are often original, relevant, central, emphatic, or indicative of the crux of argument. The fact is that a lunula marks a boundary between two textual states, one as it were the tonic, the other parenthetical to the tonic" (Lennard 242).

like a signature pattern that vividly distinguishes among writers, poets, and novelists alike.

Take Edgar Allen Poe's story "The Tell-Tale Heart" (1843), which has the uncanny effect of inducing an unreliable narrator's frenzy in the reader, with the repeated "louder" of the beating heart confusing us about whose heart it actually is. Crucially, that confusion is accentuated by punctuation even more than by syntax, as if superceding the words themselves. The dismaying indefiniteness of plot and motive, even of the narrator's gender or conceivable relationship to the victim, focuses attention on the folkloric resonances of an "evil eye," lacking rationale or explanation. Yet punctuation not only reinforces that singular absence but entombs us in the narrator's deranged mental dungeon, confronted by the analytical figures of law enforcement:

> I gasped for breath—and yet the officers heard it not. I talked more quickly—more vehemently; but the noise steadily increased. I arose and argued about trifles, in a high key and with violent gesticulations; but the noise steadily increased. Why would they not be gone? I paced the floor to and fro with heavy strides, as if excited to fury by the observations of the men—but the noise steadily increased. Oh God! what could I do? I foamed—I raved—I swore! I swung the chair upon which I had been sitting, and grated it upon the boards, but the noise arose over all and continually increased. It grew louder—louder—*louder*! And still the men chatted pleasantly, and smiled. Was it possible they heard not? Almighty God!—no, no! They heard!—they suspected!—they knew!—they were making a mockery of my horror!—this, I thought, and this I think. (Poe 233)

The strange, strained commas of "this, I thought, and this I think" seems a futile effort to reassert logical control in the midst of coming unglued—utterly unequal to the battering rhythm of delirium. The pulsating anaphora of the speaker's sentences confirms how fully the scene upends our interpretive capacities, with his panicked thoughts unsettling us through broken syntax and eerie repetitions. It is as if the dashes themselves (along with agitating exclamation points, abrupt question marks, even inflamed italics) generated the emotional panic we find ourselves feeling as we read. Clearly, one means of assessing the ratcheting up of hysteria is simply to imagine the punctuation removed, leaving syntax as is, confirming how much the text's intensity is thereby diminished.

Moreover, the invoking of punctuation as a series of regulatory policing signals has curiously merged in Poe's story with the presence of urban police themselves. It is as if the narrator were forcing the reader out of a world of conventionally trafficked meaning into the bizarre "alternative narrative universe" of punctuation described above. That effect occurs in the rising hysteria of his reaction to the policing force of the law, itself reinforced for the reader by the narrator's defiance of syntactical self-policing. Punctuation, most saliently, erupts with a proliferation of erratic em dashes, beginning by reversing possibilities, then acting as incendiary propellants. What is it about the simple line of a dash, significantly lacking an arrowhead on each end, that implies its potential to point either forward or backward? As clauses mount upon one another, the dashes appear to divide conflicting bursts of observation that reduce the prose to isolated ejaculations. The vertiginous mix of questions, exclamations, and delirious screeching is intensified inordinately by punctuation that keeps reversing and abruptly advancing, serving all by itself to confirm the horror as well as the frenzied, anxious emotional *frisson* we experience as readers.

In short, the intrigue bred by this passage lies in Poe's deliberate conjuring of a maniacal voice through little more than punctuation. And that intentional design is confirmed by contrast with his sober ratiocinative tales of detection, in their casual, otherwise sparse wielding of dashes and exclamation points. The contrast, moreover, typifies many accomplished authors, all of whom have an array of syntactical arrows in their quivers. Yet as suggested above, others sometimes come to be known for a discernable, "signature" style that persists more or less the same across a career of varied narrative efforts. By the same token, individual works can often be differentiated simply through a predilection for distinct punctuational choices. The Princeton neuroecologist Adam Calhoun has configured a series of "heat maps" of novels by stripping out words and granting a separate color for each punctuation mark (in an effort of synesthesia that serendipitously recalls Adorno's color coding: "Exclamation points are red, colons green, dashes call a halt"). Calhoun's fanciful exercise transforms Mark Twain's *Adventures of Huckleberry Finn* (1885), Virginia Woolf's *To the Lighthouse* (1927), and Cormac McCarthy's *Blood Meridian* (1985), among nearly a dozen other novels, into colorfully abstract compositions. As well, in calculating the percentage of unique marks preferred by each author, Calhoun registers statistically Faulkner's and Austen's obsession with commas in contrast to Hemingway's or McCarthy's reluctance to use subordinate or stacked clauses at all (relying instead on single-clause sentences). Striking as are the visual distinctions, however, Calhoun (like Partridge) forgoes any inclination to address the effect of such differences on readers, preferring instead merely to point them out *as* differences, perhaps arbitrary at that.[8]

The following study takes a different turn, psychologizing Calhoun's heat maps by assessing the effect on our reading of unadulterated (though as well, thoroughly adulterating) punctuation, asking what it is that writers gain in different narrative realms from different syntactic curbs. In an era of thematic surface readings, how might a look at formal infrastructure (including ligatures, disjunctures, and caesurae, if by other names) alter our understanding? What is achieved in the preference for full-stop periods instead of hypotactic clauses, for parentheses and dashes

---

[8]As Calhoun explains his color scheme: "Periods and question marks and exclamation marks are red. Commas and quotation marks are green. Semicolons and colons are blue" (Calhoun). My own preference would have been to distinguish these groupings of marks by adding more colors, and to include parentheses and em dashes. As well, question marks operate differently as a condition of dialogue between characters from a narrative pattern of punctuational emphasis.

rather than lingering commas? One might even extend the category of strictly technical punctuation to include typographical choices that achieve a similar effect: What is enacted at moments transposed into italic font or bold face that cannot be expressed by syntax alone or by conventional marks of punctuation, affectively or performatively? And why should a recent postmodernist fondness for footnotes serve narrative rhetorically, semantically, better than earlier punctuational vehicles, posing a breach in the text that finally does not derail the whole?[9] It is worth keeping in mind that when novelists aspire in their most far-flung efforts to the release of poetry, they often reveal that aspiration through the process of punctuation. What then is its aura? And why do we frequently fail to recognize its shaping power?

The question of what is gained, what lost, in the roiling possibilities of typographical marks rather than words (or rather, in conjunction *with* words) links the analyses that follow. But the rolling stakes might well be introduced by mulling over the title of John Chu's recent film, *Crazy Rich Asians* (2017). Obviously, it depends on the polysemous adjective "crazy," which could have been offered either with a hyphen ("crazy-rich," as in "impossibly rich") or with a comma ("crazy, rich," as in "whacky upper-class"). Both erase an animating ambiguity at the heart of the descriptive adjectives, with the possibility of teetering between the poles of such equivocation enlivening our reading, confirming in turn the aptness of the chosen title. Hesitating before the unsettling absence of punctuation, we skip mentally among alternate possibilities, first with comma, then hyphen—which happily, in the order it happens, clarifies the ordering of chapters below.

After all, as John Lennard has established historically, the initial punctuation to emerge after paragraphing was the period, followed

---

[9]Though footnotes, here self-consciously acknowledged in a footnote, are more palimpsists (following Gérard Genette's distinction) than actual punctuation. One need look little further than Junot Díaz, Dave Eggers, or David Foster Wallace to register how fictional footnotes seem to extend Faulkner's more abrupt interruptions of reading time and authorial presence, serving as diversion from a distinct narrative trajectory.

by commas, helping confirm their priority. And that evolution nicely corresponds to Jennifer DeVere Brody's strategic effort "to encourage readers to be attuned to punctuation's contradictory performances" (Brody 4). Analytically, Brody evaluates standard uses of punctuation marks on an arbitrary scale patterned to general usage, with the period valued as a ten against parentheses at a one, and arrayed between: commas (two); dashes (three to five); semicolons (six); and colons (eight) (Brody 136). Another way to configure the scale is to acknowledge the period as the simplest (most minimal) punctuation mark, with parentheses among the more complicated of digressions, indicating why the following chapters move from Hemingway to Faulkner.

Even so, it soon becomes clear that chapter titles are mildly misleading, dramatizing effects hardly meant as exclusive to each punctuation mark. Granted, I identify certain authors with specific marks, though those marks can and do produce different effects in the work of others. And while my discussion begins with distinctive effects, it quickly broadens scope in each case to reveal how skittish punctuation can be, depending on an author's preferences and skill. Commas act one way with Baldwin, another with Cather, and a third with Nathaniel Hawthorne: a transmutation that, far from confusing matters, only underlines punctuation's mutability. As well, the focus on largely modern American authors has more to do with my own professional interests than any theoretical claim, though I willingly wander adrift to the British Virginia Woolf and the German transplant W. G. Sebald, to the Portuguese José Saramago and even Jane Austen. These divagations along the way are meant as adventures in attention rather than exhaustive analyses, floating on occasion between prose and poetry as punctuational choices lead me astray. After all, the strategy pursued in the following chapters is at the very least to address the question posed by this prologue: "What Can Punctuation Do?" The test of any success in answering it will be the kind of additional examples you as reader can provide, proving how more varied are the effects of punctuation than I have been able to show.

1
Silence: Hemingway's Periods

Start with Hemingway, always an easy punctuational target with his presumptively flat presentation. What is it about all those arbitrary periods and equally arbitrary paragraphs that so often consist of little more than a few simple sentences, each unfurling in the indicative mood? Clauses are avoided, with full stops regularly inserted in preference to more modest comma-laden pauses, establishing a signature style that flaunts its stalwart paratactic detachments, notoriously so. Midway in his career, he would admit to struggling with a style adequate to his unconventional vision, as if learning how to strip punctuation down.[1] Here is the vignette that introduces the third story in his first collection, *In Our Time* (1925), consisting of eight sentences, ballooning from seven to sixteen words and then diminished to six:

> We were in a garden in Mons. Young Buckley came in with his patrol from across the river. The first German I saw climbed up over the garden wall. We waited till he got one leg over and then potted him. He had so much equipment on and looked

[1]As Hemingway admitted less than a decade after his earliest stories: "I was trying to write then, and I found the greatest difficulty, aside from knowing truly what you really felt, rather than what you were supposed to feel and had been taught to feel, was to put down what really happened in actions; what the actual things were which produced the emotion that you experienced. In writing for a newspaper you told what happened, and with one trick and another, you communicated the feeling of something that has happened on that day; but the real thing, the sequence of motion and fact which made the feeling and which would be as valid in a year or in ten years or, with luck and if you stated it purely enough, always, was beyond me and I was working very hard to get it" (*Death* 2).

awfully surprised and fell down into the garden. Then three more came over further down the wall. We shot them. They all came just like that. (Hemingway, *In* 29)

The whole makes sense as a series of actions, but the casually dispassionate rendition has its own distinctive effect, as Thomas Strychacz observes: "we infer slaughters so frequent that either the narrator has become dehumanized or else uses a dehumanized language as a buttress against the inhuman" (Strychacz 58). The sentences move discordantly, with a newly clear-cut perspective approximated after each period, veering from "Young Buckley" to "The first German" to "We waited" to "He had so much equipment." It is as if the focus on periods to the exclusion of any other punctuation (including paragraphing) enhanced the disconnection that lies at the heart of a soldier's mid-traumatic stress syndrome. The polysyndeton of the longest sentence, moreover, offers "a mere illusion of coherence; 'and' becomes a last desperate attempt to hold together a chaos of impressions" (Strychacz 59).

Even in far less violent accounts, punctuation generates a persistent sense of fragmentation and barely suppressed anxiety. Take "Hills Like White Elephants" (1927), perhaps Hemingway's most famous story, which offers in five pages a dialogue that alternates between periods and question marks (if also an occasional comma) in flat declarative sentences that build to a powerful if elusive emotional climax. The psychological takeaway is based on two people conversing, each establishing a separate center of consciousness, offering in the conflict between assertions, questions, and denials an uneasy impasse in understanding.

"What did you say?"
"I said we could have everything."
"We can have everything."
"No, we can't."
"We can have the whole world."
"No, we can't."
"We can go everywhere."

"No, we can't. It isn't ours any more."

"It's ours."

"No, it isn't. And once they take it away, you never get it back."

"But they haven't taken it away."

"We'll wait and see." (Hemingway, "Hills" 357)

Indeed, the marked exchange itself offers something of a forced march around an unidentified dilemma, interrupted by abrupt halts, with abbreviated expressions pausing at every tenth step, as if experience were assumed to be relatively cut and dried. Punctuation here might be said to serve as a red herring, disguising the emotional depths it nonetheless evokes.

The couple's encounter speaks for itself, if reduced to a minimal style, with simple sentences attesting to all that supposedly can be expressed, though in their clipped terseness testifying to psychological abysses lurking beneath the bland tenor of the exchange. And as if confirming this state, only a few lines following the passage above, the woman pleads inexplicably, in vain: "Would you please please please please please please please stop talking?" The lexical repetitions here match a series of other restatements of full sentences, emphasizing a certain persistence matched by the woman's reluctance to feel as the man directs. And the punctuation of this late sentence likewise matches the predominance of questions traded back and forth over the whole story (with the balance tilted heavily in her favor, at seventeen versus only four for him).[2] By the end, despite mostly calm tones of voice, we sense their relationship's ultimate dissolution—that "the weaker party might be left with 'nothing,' but she has the certainty that there is 'nothing' wrong with her, and that what is wrong is, precisely, that 'nothing'" (Link 74).

---

[2] As Alex Link claims, in his analysis of the story's lexical patterns and punctuational choices: "The movement of the text from a prominence of 'want' and 'know' to one of 'realize' and 'feel' suggests that the man is not seeking a compromise, but instead a means of getting what he wants by manipulating how Jig feels and thinks" (Link 69).

Yet that sense of things is confirmed not so much by anything said or unsaid as by the stilted syntax of the final descriptive paragraph (followed by two lines of dialogue):

> He picked up the two heavy bags and carried them around the station to the other tracks. He looked up the tracks but could not see the train. Coming back, he walked through the bar-room, where people waiting for the train were drinking. He drank an Anis at the bar and looked at the people. They were all waiting reasonably for the train. He went out through the bead curtain. She was sitting at the table and smiled at him. (Hemingway, "Hills" 358)

Once again, the paratactic sequence of simple and compound sentences seems to fragment the scene rather than integrate it. And the absence of obvious linguistic seams and graduated transitions among the sentences helps create the descriptive mood that contextualizes the couple's emotional disintegration.

One further example should confirm how fully Hemingway polished a relentlessly abbreviated mode of expression, averse to pauses and self-interruption. Writing it after the initial publication of *In Our Time*, he included "On the Quai at Smyrna" as the prologue to his 1930 edition, opening with: "The strange thing was, he said, how they screamed every night at midnight. I do not know why they screamed at that time. We were in the harbor and they were all on the pier and at midnight they started screaming. We used to turn the searchlight on them to quiet them. That always did the trick" (Hemingway, *In* 11). No semicolons or colons, no dashes, just two commas (inserting a not quite needed "he said" as if parenthetically) spread over four simple sentences. Again, Hemingway's abridged syntax rarely lapses or hesitates, enforcing the familiar tight-lipped sense that more is occurring than we can see. And for that reason, we often paradoxically feel it takes longer to move through his stories than through Faulkner's, if only because an ease of entry cloaks so much of what lies in wait on the edges of expression.

Where other authors wield punctuation to alert us to strategies of disguise, of hidden psychological depths, Hemingway realizes the genuine disguise lies in the obvious: like Poe's purloined letter hidden in the supposedly simple, the apparently transparent. And in that assumption he balances us over fragile if suggestive possibilities, forced to guess at what lies within an uninflected presentation. The precipitousness of his laconic sentences, so visibly shorn of digression and amendment, stripped of hesitations (at least expressed via parentheses, dashes, or semicolons), renders the scene ineluctably there. It is as if Hemingway anticipated Isaac Babel's notorious pronouncement: "No iron can stab the heart with such force as a period put just at the right place" (Babel 331–32). Untroubled by adverbs and adjectives as well as clauses, his narratives doggedly refuse step by careful step to modify a reader's initial impressions or otherwise adjudicate among warring inferences.

Yet the very absence of punctuation in sentences as they unfold (periods, of course, excepted) dictates an unwavering rhythm paradoxically belied by vivid details. The apparently unflappable consciousness Hemingway invokes to register a scene has the effect of instilling not calm confidence but heightened anxiety. As Jeff Scheible expansively claims of periods, offering a special insight into Hemingway's style:

> In every writer's inscription of a period there is a loaded paradox: one is relieved to have completed a sentence, but in this moment of relief one confronts an anxiety that threatens to overwhelm any sense of relief its inscription might have achieved. (Does something come next or have I finished? If something comes next, what is it? Is it someone else's turn to speak? Or must I come up with something else to say?) Every period, in other words, seems to disguise at least four question marks. In this sense the period inscribes many of the same anxieties over finality that the idea of periodization does for many historians and humanists. (Scheible 50)

The "four question marks" occluded by any given period serve to underscore how finally indefinite a full stop can be. And the period-loaded conclusion to the brief "On the Quai at Smyrna" confirms what we sense in its opening lines: "You remember the harbor. There were plenty of nice things floating around in it. That was the only time in my life I got so I dreamed about things. You didn't mind the women who were having babies as you did those with the dead ones. They had them all right" (Hemingway, *In* 12).

The casual success at maintaining a terse expressive control in the face of such a scene; the paratactic resistance to any inclination to link simple sentences together; the slippage between memory and nightmarish vision coupled with a grotesque contrast of newborns and dead babies: all is conveyed through a painstaking, even systematized adherence to full stops. As Fredric Jameson provocatively declared in his doctoral dissertation, distinguishing Sartre's use of periods from other punctuation that establishes a mental pause: "The period comes as a deep silence, a consequential gap; it has something of the force of the past definite tense: after each one areas are uncovered or new things happen" (Jameson, *Sartre* 42).[3]

But Jameson then goes on to elaborate this almost rigidly un-folding "force of the past definite tense" in a way that Hemingway's early stories disclose with dramatic clarity. The sweeping consciousness of his characters seems somehow shattered into broken segments through a fragmenting punctuation:

This silence latent in the period is by no means intrinsic to it through some kind of "nature" that it might possess: its meaning is a function of its use, and the shock, the sudden break it causes, becomes easier to sense when we realize that the normal connection in this special world between straightforward

[3]Later, Jameson explicitly addressed Hemingway's stylistic preference in terms that anticipate my claim for the priority of punctuation over preconceived meaning: "one is wrong to say that Hemingway began by wishing to express or convey certain basic experiences; rather, he began by wishing to write a certain type of sentence, a kind of neutral *compte rendu* of external displacements, and very quickly he found that such a sentence could do two kinds of things well: register movement in the external world, and suggest the tension and fitful resentment between people which is intermittently expressed in their spoken comment" (Jameson, *Marxism* 411). While punctuation is not mentioned here, it is implied in Jameson's emphasis on the sentence.

sentences describing concrete actions is not the period at all but the comma. (Jameson, *Sartre* 42)[4]

Syntactical partitioning seems enforced by periods, as if they represented the divide between opposed typewriter keyboard possibilities (as Jeff Scheible has speculated): between "the uncertainty of the question mark and on its other side . . . the overpowering certainty of the exclamation mark" (Scheible 46). The surprise is that neither of those alternative marks makes an appearance in Hemingway's narrative depictions, though more than occasionally they emerge in dialogue between characters.

Even so, Hemingway resisted crossing over, suggesting that his early avoidance of commas as mere concession to connection and coherence forms in fact a deliberate strategy, with punctuation not simply reinforcing a larger thematic agenda but actively creating it. That pattern of relying upon "the shock, the sudden break" of periods would fade with his novels, even most of his later stories, perhaps in recognition of the insight Jameson observes of full stops: "It is as if the period were so strong it had to be used with care, reserved for the most significant moments, so as not to wear it out and for fear it prove too powerful for the structure it is supposed to hold together" (Jameson, *Sartre* 43–44). Just as frequent handling of unstable gelignite leads to lost fingers, so too with periods, and perhaps predictably the explosive quality of Hemingway's early prose would necessarily settle into more temperate patterns.

As well, Hemingway discovered fruitful opportunities in learning to take a more measured, somewhat lingering perspective on syntax as well as punctuation. The very expansiveness of the novel

[4]As he adds of the comma, it "has the seeds of perpetual motion within it: it connects complete sentences, lets them pile up one after another, and suggests no superior structure which would cause a period to happen at any given point, which would of itself set an end to the fissioning development" (Jameson, *Sartre* 58). By contrast, in Jameson's logic: "The colon was bounded, centripetal, moving in upon itself to vanish at a given moment; the comma has no natural term; the form which governs it is open, full of loose ends" (Jameson, *Sartre* 59).

form revealed advantages unanticipated in his initial reliance on periods. Not that his syntax needed to adjust, but he came to realize the effect of alternative ways to express both descriptive details and the emotional connotations they evoked. A relatively inconsequential moment occurs late in *The Sun Also Rises* (1926), illustrating the contrast between Hemingway's predominant styles, early and increasingly late. The fiesta at Pamplona has already lasted four days, with Pedro Romero's emotionally exhausting performance in the bullring having left Lady Brett Ashley "limp as a rag." Then a passage occurs that announces through its punctuated division into two paragraphs how differently other marks of punctuation can evoke a mood:

> In the morning it was raining. A fog had come over the mountains from the sea. You could not see the tops of the mountains. The plateau was dull and gloom, and the shapes of the trees and the houses were changed. I walked out beyond the town to look at the weather. The bad weather was coming over the mountains from the sea.
>
> The flags in the square hung wet from the white poles and the banners were wet and hung damp against the front of the houses, and in between the steady drizzle the rain came down and drove every one under the arcades and made pools of water in the square, and the streets wet and dark and deserted; yet the fiesta kept up without any pause. It was only driven under cover. (Hemingway, *Sun* 170)

Hemingway's prose sequencing is exemplary, with sentences summing up the weather in a way that evokes the listlessness Brett admittedly feels, now shared by the narrator Jake Barnes. Again, the diction throughout is elementary ("fog had come," "flags in the square," "steady drizzle"), the repetitions self-consciously iterative ("come over the mountains," "coming over the mountains"; "drove every one under," "driven under cover").

Yet what energizes the whole is the shift in internal punctuation between the paragraphs, almost as a self-conscious switch between two contrasting styles. The first paragraph relies on

short, passively constructed, indicative sentences, all punctuated by periods with the exception of a single comma to set off a
clause (again, unnecessarily). The effect of this paratactic syntax
compounded by its abrupt punctuation is to evoke an experience
fundamentally disconnected, unassimilated, emotionally null.
The one active, narrative sentence ("I walked out . . .") confirms
by contrast the tenebrous mood hanging over the passage until
we transition into the second paragraph, where repetitions are
compounded ("wet" reiterated three times; "hung" twice). Yet
everything takes place with only two periods in a syntax otherwise all but unpunctuated, as the unscrolling polysyndeton ("and
. . . and . . . and") alters the first paragraph's "dull and gloom" into a
mood that, despite the weather, proves emotionally uplifting. It is
as if the paragraphs were meant to exemplify exactly what punctuation might do, anticipating other writers below in their varied
styles. Even Hemingway's solitary semicolon here, otherwise notably rare in his prose, anticipates Woolf's usage by moving the
reader from the swelling accumulations of water (as "rain," "sea,"
"wet," "damp," "drizzle," "pools of water") across the sentence to
the safely dry emotional harbor of the fiesta once again. In this,
Hemingway might be seen as anticipating part of the trajectory of
the following chapters.

In fact, his influence can be measured by a quick glance at
(and leap forward to) Cormac McCarthy's *The Road* (2006),
which opens in prose that appears desolate, bluntly truncated,
inflected by periods (not commas), splintered into separate impressions that are the effects of a signature style: "When he woke
in the woods in the dark and the cold of the night he'd reach out
to touch the child sleeping beside him. Nights dark beyond darkness and the days more gray each one than what had gone before.
Like the onset of some cold glaucoma dimming away the world"
(McCarthy 3).[5] That unconventional means of honing his appalling narrative may best be grasped by normalizing the syntax

[5]Ashley Kunza cites McCarthy dismissively referring to punctuation (in an
interview with Oprah Winfrey) as "weird little marks" (Kunza 146).

of this apocalyptic landscape, in registering how fully the topographic and punctuational character of description have been borrowed from Hemingway.

Consider the alternative, which might be construed as undulant, even uplifting: "When he woke in the woods, in the dark and cold of the night, he'd reach out to touch the child sleeping beside him. Nights were dark beyond darkness, and the days more gray each one than what had gone before, like the onset of some cold glaucoma dimming away the world." We realize that McCarthy's stripping away of even the most modest of pauses, relying instead on abrupt full stops, effectively divests the landscape of continuity itself. The punctuated diurnal rhythms of the latter, restructured passage have been erased. Swept into the final, unyielding "onset" of an ophthalmological simile, the passage suggests how much the scene's resistance to flux depends entirely on grammatical inducement itself. That glimpse of alternative expressive possibilities confirms how far the Hemingway style can go, in giving us one of its most dramatic instances. He lays the foundations for McCarthy's own experimental triumphs, in gesturing beyond Hemingway's repudiation of falsely comforting syntax, denying the logic of sequence or integrating flow, extending literature's further embrace of a modern world as finally disconnected, arbitrary and disjointed.[6]

---

[6]A century after Hemingway, digital communication has seen a conspicuous shunning of periods, interpreted as sign of either sarcasm or anger. Anna Davies notes: "The finality of a full stop can be construed as over-assertive or even aggressive. As a result, it is becoming more common to leave the end of a communiqué with no punctuation or with an ellipsis" (Davies 10; see also Scheible 44). Gretchen McCulloch observes that "the passive-aggressive potential of the single period" began in 2013, and describes the decorum of internet communication so: "if you're writing informally and you don't want to bother deciding whether your string of words is a full sentence or merely a clausal fragment, one way to split the difference is to punctuate ambiguously—to use an ellipsis or dash" (McCulloch 113, 112; see as well Ben Crair).

2
Hesitation: Baldwin's Commas

Given the finality of periods, one might well presume that commas (*pace* Hemingway and McCarthy) offer a less abrupt, more
even-tempered breathing space, allowing a thought or event to
be extended, developed, shaped via a series of modulations and
nuanced additions. And clauses set off by commas often do have
the effect of integrating prose, setting up appositions and implicit
connections that hone a point made less effectively in a brief simple sentence. But a profusion of commas can also lend a more pre-
cipitate, less judicious cast to prose, paradoxically registering an
antithetical effect. They can alternatively weave together moods
or unsettle ideas; they have the potential to generate harmoni-
ous rhythms—or to disrupt them. As well, an intermediate effect
can be achieved, as Nicholson Baker observes of Samuel Beckett, who "spliced the phrases of *Malone Dies* and *Molloy* together
with one-size-fits-all commas, as commonplace as stones on a
beach, to achieve that dejected sort of murmured ecphonesis so
characteristic of his narrative voice" (Baker 71). Beckett was far
too inventive and experimental in his use (and abandonment) of
punctuation for this description to be exclusively true, but it does
indicate the divergent possibilities of such marks (particularly
commas) for modern writers.[1] Earlier authors were not always so

---

[1]As James Williams asserts: "Beckett saw the problem of literature as 'trying to
find a form for . . . silence'—and the particular relationship of Beckett's work to
the problems and possibilities of silence helps us to see why Beckett's punctuation
is a subject which is beginning to attract sustained critical attention. Beckett's
prose is marked throughout by attention to starting, stopping, and pausing;

self-conscious, with Charles Dickens accused of being excessively prone to "thudding commas" while Herman Melville "flung commas like darts while riding a swell at sea, and they went wide of the mark" (Norris 96, 99). As we shall see, James Baldwin inherited this propensity a full century later.

But a contemporary far more attentive than Dickens and Melville to the effect of such pauses was Nathaniel Hawthorne, whose equivocal style built on an accumulation of clauses that regularly extend yet modify, even contradict, what his sentences initially seem to proclaim. In the hesitancy of his judgments, he remains ever averse to simple declarative statements: stating something, then done with it. Indeed, his fiction reveals a constitutional inability to rest easy in ready judgments or to settle for unmodified assessments, as if ever inclined to revise his tentative angle of vision. And such nuanced responsiveness establishes characters multidimensionally, each more than the sum of separate parts, conflicted in their own way as if at war with themselves. That style is Hawthornian, evident in nearly all he wrote, though perfected in *The Scarlet Letter* (1850), in which theme, style, and overall structure converge. Each of the novel's main figures needs to disguise a private from a public self, doing so through prose resistant to stating matters unilaterally. A fundamental ambivalence characterizes Hawthorne's vision, expressed via an equivocal, oblique, comma-strewn expressive style that renders any observation uncertain, finally enigmatic. And the narrative's own self-division (with the second half repeating and inverting the first) matches the characters' own disunion, reflected in sentences that seem to back up on themselves.

The novel's opening sentence itself offers a syntactic alternative to the social consciousness ascribed to the Puritans—of their grim self-certainty, their solid conviction, their firmly black-and-

marked too by an imaginative identification with those problems of integration and disintegration which punctuation, being connective, enacts" (Williams 251). Or as he adds: "The evolution of Beckett's prose style reads like a series of experiments with the possibilities of punctuation" (Williams 254).

white construction of social reality: "A throng of bearded men, in sad-coloured garments and grey steeple-crowned hats, inter-mixed with women, some wearing hoods, and others bareheaded, was assembled in front of a wooden edifice, the door of which was heavily timbered with oak, and studded with iron spikes" (Hawthorne 45). For those attuned to punctuation, the stuttering introduction to this community reveals in its very pauses and self-corrections an alternative to the group solidarity it strives to describe. The second chapter then opens descriptively in a style that confirms what we already know:

> The grass-plot before the jail, in Prison Lane, on a certain summer morning, not less than two centuries ago, was occu-pied by a pretty large number of the inhabitants of Boston; all with their eyes intently fastened on the iron-clamped oaken door. Amongst any other population, or at a later period in the history of New England, the grim rigidity that petrified the bearded physiognomies of these good people would have augured some awful business in hand. (Hawthorne 47)

In the controlled pauses, the clauses that accumulate sentence by sentence, the unwinding discriminations that at once augment and entangle the whole: Hawthorne at once depends on commas and somehow defies them, continuing in a distinctive brand of stylistic divertissement to the end.

Notably, midway through, he tentatively, teeteringly marvels at Hester's remaining in New England:

> It might be, too,—doubtless it was so, although she hid the secret from herself, and grew pale whenever it struggled out of her heart, like a serpent from its hole,—it might be that anoth-er feeling kept her within the scene and pathway that had been so fatal. There dwelt, there trode the feet of one with whom she deemed herself connected in a union, that, unrecognized on earth, would bring them together before the bar of final judg-ment, and make that their marriage-altar, for a joint futurity of

endless retribution. Over and over again, the tempter of souls had thrust this idea upon Hester's contemplation, and laughed at the passionate and desperate joy with which she seized, and then strove to cast it from her. She barely looked the idea in the face, and hastened to bar it in its dungeon. What she compelled herself to believe—what, finally, she reasoned upon, as her motive for continuing a resident of New England—was half a truth, and half a self-delusion. (Hawthorne 72–73)

The paragraph wonderfully captures in its hesitations and apparent lapses Hester's divided feelings, her mixed reasons for having stayed and for continuing to stay, "half a truth, and half a self-delusion."

As she compels herself to fight natural impulses and discordant feelings, the narrator confirms an ambivalence that is also highly ambiguous, not fully knowable. The shady, gray self-presentation in sentences structured so thoroughly by commas confirms the tentative view of Hester that offers such multiple possibilities. Little will change between this intermediate transitional moment and the conclusion, when: "On the threshold she paused,—turned partly round,—for, perchance, the idea of entering all alone, and all so changed, the home of so intense a former life, was more dreary and desolate than even she could bear" (Hawthorne 228). Hawthorne's almost obsessively frequent commas confirm the narrator's tentativeness as he recounts events that seem to drift back and forth. Sentences open by implying positive experiences that then end confirming the contrary, denying the reader a confident interpretation. And as sentences go, so goes the novel, with characters each appearing at last at odds with their initial appearance. Commas that tend to parse sentences in conflicting ways match the persistent evocation of both characters and depictions.

Any other study than one focused on punctuation would be unlikely to pair Hawthorne with James Baldwin, though a hunch might be ventured that their shared preoccupation with outcasts and outliers drew them to the enforced hesitation of commas. Indeed, their signature styles both depend on liberal insertions of commas in prose that initially seems not to demand them. Like Hawthorne, moreover, Baldwin realizes the antipodal logic of commas, capable of both enhancing and unsettling ideas, often at the same time. He had learned the power of these rhetorical turns from his own teen-age years as a gifted Pentecostal preacher, and his earliest essays already reveal a formidable command of English prose marked by frequent pauses. His notorious 1949 polemic against Harriet Beecher Stowe's popularity a century earlier exemplifies the tendency:

> *Uncle Tom's Cabin* is a very bad novel, having, in its self-righteous, virtuous sentimentality, much in common with *Little Women*. Sentimentality, the ostentatious parading of excessive and spurious emotion, is the mark of dishonesty, the inability to feel; the wet eyes of the sentimentalist betray his aversion to experience, his fear of life, his arid heart; and it is always, therefore, the signal of secret and violent inhumanity, the mask of cruelty. (Baldwin, *Notes* 10)

And the rest of the fiery essay, still compelling today, matches punctuation with its ideological assault on all smoothly honeyed bromides, all mawkish recitals, all trite tributes. In flat-out contravention of Stowe's reductive binaries, he earnestly advocates that "only within this web of ambiguity, paradox, this hunger, danger, darkness, can we find at once ourselves and the power that will free us from ourselves" (Baldwin, *Notes* 11).

Baldwin's bold defiance of conventional assumptions—about literary performance as well as racial attitudes—came at the time as a surprise, in spurning any accommodation to Stowe's racist if nonetheless politically liberal, abolitionist stance. But consider this account from the eminent critic F. W. Dupee of later essays in *The Fire Next Time* (1963), admiring Baldwin's prose expression as inimitably his own, independent of subject matter, worthy of full citation:

> He is in love, for example, with syntax, with sentences that mount through clearly articulated stages to a resounding and

clarifying climax and then gracefully subside. For instance this one, from *The Fire Next Time*:

> Girls, only slightly older than I was, who sang in the choir or taught Sunday school, the children of holy parents, underwent, before my eyes, their incredible metamorphosis, of which the most bewildering aspect was not their budding breasts or their rounding behinds but something deeper and more subtle, in their eyes, their heat, their odor, and the inflection of their voices.

> Nobody else in democratic America writes sentences like this anymore. It suggests the ideal prose of an ideal literary community, some aristocratic France of one's dreams. (Dupee, "Baldwin")

That was a welcome accolade, as Baldwin surely felt at the time, though it leads to the playful speculation that a supposedly democratic style might be more leveling and paratactic in contrast to the aristocratic tone Dupee admires. Much as the quoted excerpt deserves "ideal" praise, however, Dupee pointedly fails to address the question of syntactical shaping itself, the hypotactic nature of the sentence he quotes, with its vivid reliance on commas for effect. Why not more of a glance at the prose rather than simply a courteous covering gesture?

Grant that Baldwin fell into this habit as a self-confessed effect of his Bible-loving youth, coupled of course with a later devotion to Henry James. And grant as well that this comma-laden habit characterizes all his writing, early and late, fictional and nonfictional, occasional essays and fire-breathing exhortations.[2]

---

[2]While Laura Fisher likewise observes this stuttering effect, she does not focus on the syntax of multiple clauses that produces it: "*Another Country* vacillates, as interlocking affiliations prove alternately reparative and profoundly destructive; the vision of urban sociality it offers hovers between promise and peril. We might say, then, that the novel's governing mood is one of uncertain potentiality, a feeling of possibility that somehow exceeds the content of the storyline" (Fisher 138). And just a glance at the opening sentences of *If Beale Street Could Talk* (1974)

Still, he realized the antithetical possibilities contained in his punctuational preference, the paradoxical counterarguments implicit in his syntactical choice, and displayed them to powerful effect at the heart of his second novel, *Giovanni's Room* (1956). The way the novel presents the anguished experience of David, a gay American white male divorced from his own body; alienated from Hella, his long-time American girlfriend; and tormented by his feelings for the young Italian, Giovanni, who falls in love with him in Paris: all this results from Baldwin's signature use of commas. Indeed, the novel's power builds from David's dismay at what seems beyond his control, unfolding through a series of flashbacks that begins with a childhood memory of having had boyhood sex with his friend Joey. Fleeing to Europe, he proposes in sexual panic to the first American woman he meets, and then feels adrift when she retreats to Spain in order to consider that proposal. In her absence, David cannot resist a passionate affair with Giovanni, though he abandons him on Hella's return. And Giovanni's murderous anguish forces a crisis in which Hella finally forsakes David on the eve of Giovanni's public execution.

The novel's vivid thematic resonances emerge from issues related to David's sexuality, which have largely focused critical efforts. But few have observed the way his narrative voice emerges in a highly punctuated style. And no one engages the alternations between his self-conscious uncertainties (evoked by comma-laden prose) and his otherwise clear-minded declarations (stated in period-pointed sentences). This becomes apparent immediately in David's first flashback to meeting Hella, filled with the self-loathing he has felt over his brief encounter with Joey: "I can see

reveals the pattern continues throughout Baldwin's career: "*I look at myself in the mirror.* I know that I was christened Clementine, and so it would make sense if people called me Clem, or even, come to think of it, Clementine, since that's my name: but they don't" (Baldwin, *Later* 369). Likewise, consider the opening of his last novel, *Just Above My Head* (1979): "The damn'd blood burst, first through his nostrils, then pounded through the veins in his neck, the scarlet torrent exploded through his mouth, it reached his eyes and blinded him, and brought Arthur down, down, down, down, down" (Baldwin, *Later* 515).

her, very elegant, tense, and glittering, surrounded by the light which fills the salon of the ocean liner, drinking rather too fast, and laughing, and watching the men. That was how I met her" (Baldwin, *Early* 222). The simple words and brief clauses cluster together, as if in pointillist representation of the past, pulling together a series of images.

Yet the staccato delivery at the same time vigorously denies such a weave, seeming ever uncertain, pausing too often, hiccuping unrestrainedly—as much in resistance to the memory as in solicitation. And on the next page, likewise, David continues to draw on associations that pull up in their own turn a flood of untoward memories:

> I was thinking, when I told Hella that I had loved her, of those days before anything awful, irrevocable, had happened to me, when an affair was nothing more than an affair. Now, from this night, this coming morning, no matter how many beds I find myself in between now and my final bed, I shall never be able to have any more of those boyish, zestful affairs—which are, really, when one thinks of it, a kind of higher, or, anyway, more pretentious masturbation. (Baldwin, *Early* 222)

"Pretentious" indeed, as the self-involved, onanistic musings confirm, though punctuation again shapes recollection into a series of mixed moments, of clashing feelings, present and past, with mere masturbatory release shackled syntactically together with a profound and redeeming affection. We are hard-pressed to separate out the diverse moments, in the alignment of "boyish, zestful affairs" somehow with "an affair," simple and heteronormative. Unlike any other writer, Baldwin evokes through commas a deeply contradictory state of mind that perfectly embodies David's consciousness, torn between what he thinks he wants and what his body actually desires and says to him. In this regard, Baldwin's perspective aligns with Hawthorne's.

Even in more self-contained, self-satisfied moments, David's syntax doubles back, appearing to reverse itself, though the commas (rather than dashes, say) suggest the reversals are only meant to be momentary, without any deeper reconsideration or a fuller plan of revision:

> Then I, alone, and relieved to be alone, perhaps went to a movie, or walked, or returned home and read, or sat in a park and read, or sat on a café terrace, or talked to people, or wrote letters. I wrote to Hella, telling her nothing, or I wrote to my father asking for money. And no matter what I was doing, another me sat in my belly, absolutely cold with terror over the question of my life. (Baldwin, *Early* 287)

The recurrent "or"s pepper a prose that seems in the first two sentences to lack direction before the third reveals a self-loathing that regularly nullifies any activity, unravels any coherent state of mind, invalidates any feeling of integrated selfhood.

Even in less taut situations, David's thoughts rarely cohere, as if his emotional register were—in good times or bad, wrought moments or calm—invariably perturbed, unfocused, lacking concentration:

> The bus came and the policeman and I, the only people waiting, got on—he stood on the platform, far from me. The policeman was not young, either, but he had a gusto which I admired. I looked out of the window and the streets rolled by. Ages ago, in another city, on another bus, I sat so at the windows, looking outward, inventing for each flying face which trapped my brief attention some life, some destiny, in which I played a part. I was looking for some whisper, or promise, of my possible salvation. (Baldwin, *Early* 340–41)

Here, simply boarding a bus, casting his eyes about, David lapses into a fractured mental syntax, unable to string together observations into the polysyndeton of a calmly tranquil stream of consciousness. Instead, commas mandate a wild looking before and after, as if not simply allowing us to be swept along unwaveringly but imploring us to pause at the same time to look further ahead, then behind, before continuing with the sentence.

Moreover, confirming that this is not simply an unthinking signature style, unvaried in any and all situations, Baldwin invokes a very different expressive mode for Hella when she finally can no longer endure David's inexplicable behavior: "Please. I want to go home. I want to get married. I want to start having kids. I want us to live someplace, I want *you*. Please David. What are we marking time over here for?" (Baldwin, *Early* 353). The short anaphoric sentences, isolated by abrupt, seemingly stalwart periods that articulate her coldly angry, anguished state, reinforce a difference from David, contrasting her knowledge of what it is she actually does want with the kind of relationship she still desires, if irredeemably.

By contrast, David continues as if unassuaged, even in the midst of her faltering final kiss: "It seemed that my body, next to her warmth, her insistence, under her hands, would never awaken. But when it awakened, I had moved out of it. From a great height, where the air all around me was colder than ice, I watched my body in a stranger's arms" (Baldwin, *Early* 353). Again, the customary weight of commas is light, continuing an idea, enhancing a formulation; but Baldwin's intense rhetorical practice tends to have the opposite effect—making us self-conscious as readers about what is *not* being protracted and conjoined but instead paused, even reversed. And as we shall see, punctuational reversals are more often the domain of dashes than commas, though it may not come as surprise that writers drawn to one have frequently been inclined toward the other. And even when not—when a preference for dashes conspicuously outweighs other punctuational choices, as in the case of Emily Dickinson or Henry James—editors have more than occasionally intervened to replace the dashes with commas.

That species of intervention makes it appropriate here to pause over Jane Austen, especially since she represents a quandary for editors eager to correct her punctuational style—one that teeters, as we do at the moment, between commas and dashes. Clearly, Austen offers a glaring contrast to Baldwin: not only for obvious thematic differences; nor because early nineteenth-century standards for punctuation were not yet prescribed; nor even because of our uneasiness about her punctuational intentions (possibly altered, possibly confirmed by editors, leaving us uncertain in the absence of original manuscripts); but because of her eccentric writing style itself. "Her style is much more intimate and relaxed, more conversational," Kathryn Sutherland argues; "Her punctuation is much more sloppy, more like the kind of thing our students do and we tell them not to. She uses capital letters and underlining to emphasise the words she thinks important, in a manner that takes us closer to the speaking voice than the printed page. In taking them away, it becomes more grammatical and sophisticated—but something has been lost" (cited by Maev Kennedy). As another critic observes, "Austen hardly punctuates at all, so what you get is a much more urgent form of language which becomes more restrained when it is edited. There tends to be an awful lot of clauses and sub-clauses. There is the odd comma, but they aren't always in the most rational places. There are no paragraphs" (Malvern).

The controversy over Austen's punctuation has recently aroused scholars and critics unsettled by Sutherland's claims, though one of the examples she offers nicely suggests the stakes involved. The only surviving manuscript fragment available for Austen is a revised section of her late novel *Persuasion* (1817), preserved simply because it was canceled and replaced. Yet it gives a vivid sense of her typical offhand style, evident in private letters that rely on frequent capitalizations and clearly tilt toward dashes[3]:

> "When I yeilded [*sic*], I thought it was to Duty.—But no Duty could be called in aid here.—In marrying a Man indifferent to me, all Risk would have been incurred, & all Duty violated."—

[3]Sutherland identifies one prominent editor as the "notoriously pedantic" William Gifford (Sutherland, *Textual* 303). Of alterations in the second edition of *Mansfield Park*, she adds that "the majority of changes do not suggest authorial polish; rather, they indicate the routine readying of manuscript for publication by an external hand" (*Textual* 159). Five years later, under attack for this interpretation, Sutherland quoted from Gifford's letters to reveal how vexed he was by Austen's punctuation (see Sutherland, "Austen's").

"Perhaps I ought to have reasoned thus, he replied, but I could not.—I could not derive benefit from the later knowledge of your Character which I had acquired, I could not bring it into play, it was overwhelmed, buried, lost in those earlier feelings, which I had been smarting under Year after Year.—" (Sutherland, "Austen's")

This is the way Austen penned the manuscript, with neither line breaks nor paragraph indentations, presumably in order to economize on expensive writing paper.[4] And here is the printed version, where changes that seem small prove cumulatively significant:

"When I yielded, I thought it was to duty; but no duty could be called in aid here. In marrying a man indifferent to me, all risk would have been incurred, and all duty violated."

"Perhaps I ought to have reasoned thus," he replied, "but I could not. I could not derive benefit from the late knowledge I had acquired of your character. I could not bring it into play: it was overwhelmed, buried, lost in those earlier feelings which I had been smarting under year after year." (Sutherland, "Austen's")

That is, Austen's printed use of commas or dashes (as much as quotation marks, capitalization, and paragraphing) would seem to have been as much a copy editor's determination as her own, always assuming that she approved of the amendments.

Another way to describe the finished effect is that an "intention" in the text seems to fly free of the author, or at least is not entirely circumscribed by her original inclination. Austen's hand-

---

[4]As Sutherland reminds us, the exchanges between characters can appear in her published novels as an "exaggeratedly staccato performance," back and forth: "It is tempting to invoke at this point the evidence of the extant manuscripts, where paragraphing is far more fluid than print conventions normally allow. But the manuscripts are not reliable as an indicator of Austen's print intentions since, as in the cancelled fragment of *Persuasion*, for example, there is no paragraphing of any kind throughout a whole chapter" (Sutherland, *Textual* 309).

written sentences, Jenny Davidson observes, "are spikier, more idiosyncratic than anything we see in her novels as they have been printed," even though she admits, "It is an illusion of sorts, as the sequence of words is identical" (Davidson 36). That domesticating impulse (of generally removing dashes from prose) became more apparent through the course of the century, though our sense of the "polite" rhythm of Austen's printed novels is dramatically enhanced by realizing how fully her own voice sounds so dynamic, even bristling; expressively, in terms of punctuational conventions, it might be said that she "looks backward rather than forward" (Davidson 37).

Still, Sutherland poses an interesting question for the intersection of punctuational choice and mediated expression in Austen's later work:

> What these occasions for mistaken editorial conjecture hold in common is a quality characteristic of Austen's mature narrative style which can be described as vocal encroachment. It is most famously present in those passages in which a central fictional consciousness (usually female, often the heroine's) is absorbed into the omniscient narrator's voice, a fusion of first- and third-person narrative, usually designated "free indirect discourse." The skill of such a method lies in its compression, and in particular in the overlaying of one voice by another. It is at just such moments, when the text is most richly and at the same time least precisely voiced, that it betrays the logic of the reading eye and denies its visual confinement. (Sutherland, *Textual* 300)

Compounding the issue is that we have no available evidence for Austen's influence on her novels' repunctuation. Sutherland sides against authorial revision in favor of its being a decision made by others on behalf of the printing house, though Rachel Brownstein offers a perfectly reasonable retort that nothing precludes Austen's having made her own corrections to manuscripts sent to the printer.

Perhaps less important than why dashes may have been expunged is the fact that those remaining have so decided an effect, sometimes merely standing in for commas or semicolons, at others suggesting a character's heightened emotional turmoil, at still others a helter-skelter mental chaos. In each case, the momentary conversational breach in an em dash registers an intensifying disruption of thought. Among the more notorious splashes of such punctuation in *Emma* occurs in the outing to Mr. Knightley's estate at Donwell Abbey, where Emma takes in the "becoming characteristic situation," observing to herself: "—It was just what it ought to be, and it looked what it was—and Emma felt an increasing respect for it" (Austen 335, 336). Gradually, swept up by dashes into the scene of strawberry picking, Emma's inner thoughts merge with dialogue both spoken and heard:

> and Mrs. Elton, in all her apparatus of happiness, her large bonnet and her basket, was very ready to lead the way in gathering, accepting, or talking—strawberries, and only strawberries, could now be thought or spoken of.—"The best fruit in England—every body's favourite—always wholesome.—These the finest beds and finest sorts.—Delightful to gather for one's self—the only way of really enjoying them.—Morning decidedly the best time—never tired—every sort good—hautboy infinitely superior—no comparison—the others hardly eatable—hautboys very scarce—Chili preferred—white wood finest flavour of all—price of strawberries in London—abundance about Bristol—Maple Grove—cultivation—beds when to be renewed—gardeners thinking exactly different—no general rule—gardeners never to be put out of their way—delicious fruit—only too rich to be eaten much of—inferior to cherries—currants more refreshing—only objection to gathering strawberries the stooping—glaring sun—tired to death—could bear it no longer—must go and sit in the shade." (Austen 335)

Initially, the passage seems to become a monologue by the pretentious Mrs. Elton, though in the very next line the narrator affirms, "Such, for half an hour, was the conversation" (Austen 335).

In fact the dash-laden "conversation," we now realize, may be not only Mrs. Elton droning on but others breaking in, offering interjections (signaled by silent dashes) to which she responds, or perhaps even sneaking in on Emma's own private thoughts. Voice itself becomes confused (is it Mrs. Elton? others in the party? even the narrator?), with the reader offered snatches at once shaped by Emma's introductory thoughts, perhaps even her sly mimicry, thus offording a more nuanced view of the heroine's shifting response than we had at first surmised. Here as elsewhere, Austen's proclivity for dashes allows a heightened response to a scene that plays out dramatically, but also emotionally, with dialogue internalized. The question left standing, certainly following the example of Hawthorne and Baldwin, is whether these dashes (as so many others in Austen's manuscripts) might readily have been replaced by the commas that copy editor William Gifford desired. Perhaps so, though it is worth keeping in mind how conventional formal attitudes toward the em dash would change.

3
Interruption: James's Dashes

Before turning to Henry James's altered mastery of dashes a century later, we might recall the various uses to which they had already been put: according to Ben Yagoda, a "mark that—unlike commas, periods, semicolons and all the others—doesn't seem to be subject to any rules" (Yagoda).[1] Poe had drawn on the em dash as a means of imparting a certain frenzy, but even earlier Washington Irving had turned to dashes in "Rip Van Winkle" (1819),

---

[1]Prior to Austen, the most prominent virtuoso of dashes was Laurence Sterne in *The Life and Opinions of Tristram Shandy* (1759–67). As John Lennard observes, however, they also function (like Austen's) idiosyncratically: "the sense of Tristram's personality, character, and mental habits which his text produces is mediated largely through the broken-dash'd and parenthetic appearance of the *mise-en-page*. Digressions operate at all levels in *Tristram Shandy*, including those of the chapter and the volume, but they are manifest in the dashes and lunulae which spatter each page of text" (Lennard 140). As he adds of Tristram, "The ruling characteristics of that mind it would be hard to pin down—speculative, restless, impatient of restraint, passionately enamoured of words and devoted to the pursuit of ideas, but apt to pursue them for their appeal to the imagination rather than for their claims upon the intellect" (Lennard 141). Roger Moss had earlier observed, "Indeed, what we should see is that digressions themselves are 'things' just as much as they are responses to feeling. No reader of Sterne should fall into the trap of reading the book as a series of digressions, following each one with the seriousness that the surface demands—that is, following them 'straightforwardly'—and forgetting that digression is an issue in the book as well as a technique. Digression is an object standing in the way of narrative as much as it is an adjunct to narrative—it is 'thing' as much as 'feeling,' 'body' as much as 'mind'" (Moss 186).

when the titular figure awakens in the Catskills after a twenty-year slumber:

> "Surely," thought Rip, "I have not slept here all night." He recalled the occurrences before he fell asleep. The strange man with a keg of liquor—the mountain ravine—the wild retreat among the rocks—the woe begone party at ninepins—the flagon—"ah! that flagon! that wicked flagon!" thought Rip—"what excuse shall I make to Dame Van Winkle?" (Irving 776)

His befuddlement as he remembers the moments immediately prior to falling asleep is manifested via the same punctuation that in Poe marked the narrator's hysterical state, which in turn induces a similar sense of convulsive horror in the reader.

Later, when Rip at last returns home to find all utterly transformed, the dashes crowd in once again to register his amazed emotional state:

> The very village was altered—it was larger and more populous. There were rows of houses which he had never seen before, and those which had been his familiar haunts had disappeared. Strange names were over the doors—strange faces at the windows—every thing was strange. His mind now misgave him . . . There stood the Kaatskill mountains—there ran the silver Hudson at a distance—there was every hill and dale precisely as it had always been—Rip was sorely perplexed—"That flagon last night," thought he,—"has addled my poor head sadly!" (Irving 778)

Where another author might have relied on commas or semicolons, the effect of this alternative punctuation is to ratchet up consternation, to amplify Rip's disorientation, to more actively isolate disconnected impressions and observations from each another as a means of simulating his befuddled state of mind.

Henry James, more than any previous author, understood the diverse emotive possibilities embodied in the em dash, building on his predecessors' use of them for emotional self-division, intellectual reconsideration, and digressive heightening, but incorporating the horizontal mark to different ends in ways that establish it as his dominant punctuational mode.[2] Nor was this an understanding acquired gradually, but apparently an insight intuited very early. Indeed, his first interview in 1881 began with a reporter's asking "if certain words just used should be followed by a dash, and even boldly added: 'Are you not famous, Mr. James, for the use of dashes?'"[3]

Famous or not, James was clearly drawn to dramas of psychological wavering, to a process of thinking that resists straightforward unfolding and instead appears broken, as sedimented images and ideas about one another, with psychological landscapes tilted awry by verbal plate tectonics. And to see the imprint of punctuation over his sentences, we realize the "dash man" is certainly that, if also much more. The dash, as it were, comes to encapsulate James's entire stylistic revolution, signaling a need to make an abrupt stop, to pause in whiplash style, to consider the pull of possible diversions in the very presentation of diversion

---

[2] It is worth noting the dubious status of the dash in modern writing, contrary to its standing with Austen and her contemporaries. As W. S. Maugham observed: "There is in the dash something rough, ready and haphazard that goes against my grain. I have seldom read a sentence in which it could not be well replaced by the elegant semi-colon or the discreet bracket" (Carey 20). For an alternative view, see Yagoda.

[3] One should not be surprised to learn that James was justly self-conscious about his punctuational reputation:

"Dash my fame!" he impatiently replied. "And remember, please, that dogmatizing about punctuation is exactly as foolish as dogmatizing about any other form of communication with the reader. All such forms depend on the kind of thing one is doing and the kind of effect one intends to produce. Dashes, it seems almost platitudinous to say, have their particular representative virtue, their quickening force, and, to put it roughly, strike both the familiar and the emphatic note, when those are the notes required, with a felicity beyond either the comma or the semicolon; though indeed a fine sense for the semicolon, like any sort of sense at all for the pluperfect tense and the subjunctive mood, on which the whole perspective in a sentence may depend, seems anything but common. Does nobody ever notice the calculated use by French writers of a short series of suggestive points in the current of their prose? I confess to a certain shame for my not employing frankly that shade of indication, a finer shade still than the dash." (Lockwood)

---

itself. Few other writers have so persistently represented con-sciousness as multiple, undecided, conflated, interrupting delibe-ration with interjections—and realized that the only way to represent this syntactically was through the em dash. As typo-graphic lines that point both forward and backward, dashes rep-resent a breaking off, or a turning to some prior moment or state of belief, or simply an effort to start anew, in anticipation of fresh possibilities.[4] James's narratives embody in that regard a Hamlet-like hesitation, frequently reviewing what has occurred and what might have occurred in its stead, all to explore possibilities that exceed whatever his narrative exposes as having in fact occurred (which can prove a more interesting narrative).

Perhaps unsurprisingly, the em dash was not something James reserved for his novels alone; indeed, it seems to have been a central intellectual lever for him—part of the way in which he translated impressions into symbolic form. Mark Boren has completed a thorough investigation of notes that James made to himself, and nicely focuses upon sheer grammatical marks: "In James's original notebooks . . . horizontal lines abound: lines run between words; lines run beneath them. The visual impact of his ubiquitous lines (in the original notebooks) is inescapable. They delineate thoughts, break apart clauses, underscore ideas, and give emphasis" (Boren 330). And that inescapable pattern of lines scrawled across a page, forming an iconic representation of the mental elisions and delays he himself experienced, defined in his early years the initial patterns of thought that would in more elaborate configurations come to characterize his later fictional triumphs.

---

[4]Theodor Adorno observed: "To the person who cannot truly conceive anything as a unit, anything that suggests disintegration or discontinuity is unbearable; only a person who can grasp totality can understand caesuras. But the dash provides instruction in them. In the dash, thought becomes aware of its fragmentary character. It is no accident that in the era of the progressive degeneration of language, this mark of punctuation is neglected precisely insofar as it fulfills its function: when it separates things that feign a connection. All the dash claims to do now is to prepare us in a foolish way for surprises that by that very token are no longer surprising" (Adorno 302).

Yet the editorial translations made of James's notebooks are themselves revelatory of the ways in which cultural dictates and conventional mores could so easily transform meaning itself. As Boren goes on to explain, in describing the nonverbal but importantly visual and iconic status of James's dashes:

> When his notebooks are eventually published, thirty-one years after his death, the countless dashes make it into the published notes, but the copious underlining is translated into italics. The bold editorial act of italicization maintains the stress placed on select words, but it destroys an important facet of James's notes: the sheer number of horizontal lines traversing his text and thus the significance he placed on the physical line itself. In viewing the original notes, the impression one has, the visual image inscribed on one's retinas and in one's brain, is of an almost illegible scrawl punctuated by a plethora of horizontal lines. Obviously (in the original notebooks) the horizontal flourish is essential to James's thought processes. Emphases certainly survive in the translation for publication—on those words that are italicized—but what is lost is the significance attached to "the line." In James's original notebooks, the horizontal line is unmistakable and therefore significant. (Boren 330)

Intriguingly, James perceives narrative as fully a graphic as a symbolic form, with meaning registered through the kind of icons that Faulkner would later include directly in his novels (of pictorial eyes or coffins, or simply of empty spaces—all meant as actual physical depictions rather than verbal representations).[5]

As early as "Daisy Miller" (1879), James had embraced the dash's oral tonality, in the doubling back and leaping forward that reminds us of someone in the midst of thinking while speaking.

---

[5]This concern with marks on a page not as signs but as something more like drawings is central to current critical interpretation of Emily Dickinson, led by the intervention of Susan Howe's *The Birth-Mark*. Further discussion of this issue is pursued later in this chapter.

Of course, the move from iconic (visual, graphic) punctuation to its oral effects suggests a twofold, rabbit-duck conflation hard to experience at the same time, as lines across a page transform both speaker and reader into stuttering uncertainty. The novella's opening paragraph delights in crisscrossed clauses divided by commas, with a slightly pretentious narrator offering a tourist's guide to Vevey. But then suddenly, the second paragraph dives into dashes:

> He had come from Geneva the day before by the little steamer, to see his aunt, who was staying at the hotel—Geneva having been for a long time his place of residence. But his aunt had a headache—his aunt had almost always a headache—and now she was shut up in her room, smelling camphor, so that he was at liberty to wander about. He was some seven-and-twenty years of age; when his friends spoke of him, they usually said that he was at Geneva "studying." When his enemies spoke of him, they said—but, after all, he had no enemies; he was an extremely amiable fellow, and universally liked. What I should say is, simply, that when certain persons spoke of him they affirmed that the reason of his spending so much time at Geneva was that he was extremely devoted to a lady who lived there—a foreign lady—a person older than himself. Very few Americans—indeed, I think none—had ever seen this lady, about whom there were some singular stories. But Winterbourne had an old attachment for the little metropolis of Calvinism; he had been put to school there as a boy, and he had afterward gone to college there—circumstances which had led to his forming a great many youthful friendships. (James, *Turn* 269)

Clearly, the narrator has shifted from the cumulative tempo of the opening, in its slyly patronizing if practiced patter of setting a scene, to this acquired portrait of Winterbourne, whom we soon learn is as full of brusque conclusions as the punctuated description anticipates. Instead of calm formulations, this dash-laden sequence pivots nervously, adding details belatedly, self-correctively, seeming in the process a bit distracted. It is as if

Winterbourne himself were here displacing the narrator's cultured tentativeness, his largely conditional tone, as the narrative quietly adopts Winterbourne's less judicious reliance on binary thinking. And curiously, this clotting of dashes largely disappears from the story as Winterbourne's own emergent first-person voice makes such narrative seesawing unnecessary.[6]

Dashes would accompany James throughout his career, predictably and sardonically appearing at the onset of *In the Cage* (1898), set in a telegraph office where the Morse-coded communication of electrical pulses is slyly inserted as dots and dashes into the novella. There, they provide a textual (and punctuational) context for the mysterious narrative:

> It had occurred to her early that in her position—that of a young person spending, in framed and wired confinement, the life of a guinea-pig or a magpie—she should know a great many persons without their recognising the acquaintance. That made it an emotion the more lively—though singularly rare and always, even then, with opportunity still very much smothered—to see any one come in whom she knew outside, as she called it, any one who could add anything to the meanness of her function. Her function was to sit there with two young men—the other telegraphist and the counter-clerk. (James, *Cage* 174)

And dashes (as well as full-stopped dots) continue through nearly every paragraph that ensues, as if to punctuate a theme that relies on enigmatic communications duly tapped out yet tantalizingly incomprehensible to the female telegraph operator who sends them.

---

[6]Robin Riehl has studied James's editing of this story in 1909, focusing on the dropped commas intended to disambiguate the whole: "James's injunction suggests that his 'no-commas' and other punctuation changes are indeed 'essential' to reading his revised text. Close examination of revised passages shows that the pervasively altered punctuation serves much more than a stylistic purpose: it is neither accidental nor irrelevant to readings of the revised text" (Riehl 69). Yet the dashes remain largely intact.

By the time of *The Ambassadors* (1903) five years later, James had mastered what earlier seemed mildly experimental, though his pattern of introducing dashes is similar.[7] The novel's opening paragraph has three pointed interruptions of the narrative voice itself, but this pattern only really gets going in the second paragraph:

> That note had been meanwhile—since the previous afternoon, thanks to this happier device—such a consciousness of personal freedom as he hadn't known for years; such a deep taste of change and of having above all for the moment nobody and nothing to consider, as promised already, if headlong hope were not too foolish, to colour his adventure with cool success. There were people on the ship with whom he had easily consorted—so far as ease could up to now be imputed to him—and who for the most part plunged straight into . . . (James, *Ambassadors* 22)

Here, Strether's consciousness is represented via a combination of commas and dashes, of sequences sutured together that gradually build, then abruptly interrupt themselves, as thoughts are elaborated and subsequently corrected. Indeed, one might well presume that James's central theme has caught up to his style, with the opening hesitations of "Daisy Miller" reflecting a savvy narrator hedging his bets, now transformed into the basis of plot itself. The focus on Strether is on a consciousness always teetering between certainty and reformulation, ever ready to reconsider its own premises on the other side of a dash. The "stiff" psychology informing the earlier narrative that skewers a flirtatious Daisy Miller has now become the flexible, earnest, responsive

---

[7] In 1897, James began dictating his fiction and memoirs, with careful instructions for where and what sort of punctuation he intended. As his typewriting amanuensis, Theodora Bosanquet, later described: "The spelling out of the words, the indication of commas, were scarcely felt as a drag on the movement of his thought. 'It all seems,' he once explained, 'to be so much more effectively and unceasingly pulled out of me in speech than in writing'" (Bosanquet 34).

consciousness that wants to understand what has become of Chad Newsome.[8]

And while many of the novel's dashes occur as acoustic gestures, endeavoring to capture the quality of spoken conversation with its back and forth reversals, just as many occur narratively in Strether's self-conscious realization of how little he actually knows, or can otherwise depend upon. Again, the potential distinction between oral and visual makes the prose resonate, as pictorial and symbolic representations vie with each other:

> It was positively droll to him that he should already have Maria Gostrey, whoever she was—of which he hadn't really the least idea—in a place of safe keeping. He had somehow an assurance that he should carefully preserve the little token he had just tucked in. He gazed with unseeing lingering eyes as he followed some of the implications of his act, asking himself if he really felt admonished to qualify it as disloyal. It was prompt, it was possibly even premature, and there was little doubt of the expression of face the sight of it would have produced in a certain person. But if it was "wrong"—why then he had better not have come out at all. At this, poor man, had he already—and even before meeting Waymarsh—arrived. (James, *Ambassadors* 26)

Regularly, the narrative voice is broken up by dashes that establish how little Strether can confidently assume or assert. Stymied, halting, uncertain how to continue, he characteristically

---

[8]According to Mark Boren:

> There are 2325 dashes in *The Ambassadors*. This multitude is not surprising though, considering that the text itself revolves around the presence, or absence, of significance in life and the "undecidability" of communication. In rendering the protagonist's difficulty in negotiating the world and his hesitancy to enter into it, and in highlighting the constant attempts at communication between characters and the inevitable misunderstandings and misreadings that result, Henry James wields the dash to amazing effect. (Boren 338)

interrupts himself in almost any verbal gesture. Or as he queries
Maria Gostrey, "Well, is Chad—what shall I say?—monstrous?"
almost as if the words "what shall I say?" do little more than du-
plicate the meaning of the dashes themselves (James, *Ambassadors* 116).

Moreover, at moments like this, we sometimes pause to
consider the difference between the parenthetical dash in mid-
sentence (as here, which actually constitutes two sets of dashes)
and other varieties: the multiple dashes in "The Tell-Tale Heart,"
say, which attest to a hysterical consciousness, or those single
dashes that otherwise end a sentence, signaling something yet
unstated. Here, Strether's self-impeding flow turns from the
merely querulous to something more revelatory of his questing
intelligence, as he realizes once again how little his own bland
assumptions cover the facts of the case he desperately wants to
understand.

Near the end of the novel, wandering outside Paris into the
countryside, Strether lets his imagination wander as well:

> He really continued in the picture—that being for himself
> his situation—all the rest of this rambling day; so that the
> charm was still, was indeed more than ever upon him when,
> toward six o'clock, he found himself amicably engaged with
> a stout white-capped deep-voiced woman at the door of the
> *auberge* of the biggest village, a village that affected him as a
> thing of whiteness, blueness and crookedness, set in coppery
> green, and that had the river flowing behind or before it—one
> couldn't say which. (James, *Ambassadors* 415)

Again, the syntax converges on the dash that finally covers the
scene, providing the fullest description only to end in quizzical
uncertainty that suggests how little optical clarity is ever clear.
And as the scene unfolds in shocked surprise at what has actually
become of Chad, dashes erupt dramatically. The point is that Strether's signature style, the way in which his discernibly heightened
consciousness manifests itself, is *through* his punctuation.

A year later, "The Beast in the Jungle" (1903) presents John Marcher persistently anticipating that his life will pass him by somehow unlived. Yet ironically, it is he who drains that life away in obsessive anticipation, refusing the patient love of his one close friend, ever holding out for something yet to come rather than already here in the person of May Welland: devoted, faithful, already happening as he awaits. By the end of the story, what remains is a stymied sense of life blocked by punctuation, with dashes prominent but compounded as well by semicolons, parentheses, periods: all representing the psychological resistances he has suffered, from which he had never been able to break free into sinuously self-possessed, unremitting, and integrated prose. Again, the reader feels frustrated as much by halting exposition as with an obstructed consciousness, contributing as fully to a desire for stylistic release as for psychological deliverance:

> The escape would have been to love her; then, *then* he would have lived. *She* had lived—who could say now with what passion?—since she had loved him for himself; whereas he had never thought of her (ah how it hugely glared at him!) but in the chill of his egotism and the light of her use. Her spoken words came back to him—the chain stretched and stretched. (James, *Turn* 481)

Apart from the parenthetical self-laceration of "(ah how it hugely glared at him!)," itself intensified by that exclamation point, consider how the dashes in this long sentence tend to break the pace, contributing to the emotional devastation of Marcher's regret. Looking back and then despairingly forward along the "chain" of moments locking him into the present he now suffers, we realize how much that condition has been elicited by dashes. Their effect is to puncture a sustainable rhythm, to break off an associative progression, to sideline a thought or reduce an experience into something else entirely.

In fact, much of the story prepares for this end, relying on dashes from the opening sentence, as if to anticipate a life that will defy continuity or sequence. Instead, Marcher remains inert, paralyzed, condemned to starting ever anew (or rather, never able to actually start). His meeting with May Bartram at the country house at Weatherend becomes at once a premonition and a perpetuation, reflected in its punctuation: "They lingered together still, she neglecting her office—for from the moment he was so clever she had no proper right to him—and both neglecting the house, just waiting as to see if a memory or two more wouldn't again breathe on them" (James, *Turn* 328). Thereafter, their relationship is marked by a regularly broken rhythm that captures his haunted dread of being utterly isolated:

> He had thought of himself so long as abominably alone, and lo he wasn't alone a bit. He hadn't been, it appeared, for an hour—since those moments on the Sorrento boat. It was she who had been, he seemed to see as he looked at her—she who had been made so by the graceless fact of his lapse of fidelity. To tell her what he had told her—what had it been but to ask something of her? (James, *Turn* 331)

The dashes here all but implement Marcher's narcissism, returning him ever back to a moment that should supposedly confirm his presupposition, rather than opening out to some newer, more reflective progression of linked, integrated scenes.[9]

By the time he asks that question, midway through, the hoped-for solution already seems helplessly belated. Anticipation itself has become simply a reconsideration: "What did everything mean—what, that is, did she mean, she and her vain waiting and

[9]It is worth noting how, in contrast to his reliance on dashes, James never uses an ellipsis. That may be explained by Adorno's claim that "The ellipsis, a favorite way of leaving sentences meaningfully open during the period when Impressionism became a commercialized mood, suggests an infinitude of thoughts and associations" (Adorno 303). That very "infinitude" is precisely what James would deny as the interesting psychological strain in his characters. By contrast, Jennifer DeVere Brody more tautly declares: "The ellipsis can stand for what *need not be said*, for what may be redundant to say as well as for what *cannot be said*, for that which exceeds locution and is therefore impossible" (Brody 77).

her probable death and the soundless admonition of it all—unless that, at this time of day, it was simply, it was overwhelmingly too late?" (James, *Turn* 347). And May's own reassuring confirmation that "It's never too late" (James, *Turn* 353) serves not to clarify but to confuse our reading, injecting doubt into any assurance that Marcher has at last grasped the futility of his life. We end (as does he, it seems) unsure of how to read his fate, as either further condemnation of a life lived with consummate egotism or a transformation of consciousness in which he at last sees what was wrong in his stuttering, stifling choices all along. A large part of that closing confusion emerges from James's punctuational finesse, having transfigured through his "use of dashes" (already notorious early on) the simple confusions of "Daisy Miller" into the far more complex psychological troublings of a life held at a stammering pause.[10] The dash, in short, might well be thought of as emblem of Marcher's fate.

[10]As if to clarify James's distinctive tone, consider Max Beerbohm's notorious parody, which strangely favors an unusually energetic comma over the more characteristic dash in a way that makes Jamesian prose seem fussier and more ingrown, if also finally not quite familiar. http://www.parodies.org.uk/james-be erbohm.htm

4
Rupture: Dickinson's Dashes

The ever-present question of what sort of pause to invoke—whether the calm interlude of a comma, the suspension of a parenthesis, the hitch of a semicolon, or the caesura of a dash—is always at once consequence and cause of an author's signature vision. Achieving a certain prescribed pacing of expression is dictated as much by the choice among such options as by larger syntactical arrangements or thematic adjustments. Yet the choice is not always clear at first to the reader, and rarely becomes a dilemma once a story or poem has been published. This makes the notorious history of Emily Dickinson's edited poems a particularly revelatory one, of typography interrupted in the standoff between supposedly presumptuous dashes replaced by acquiescent commas. Her nearly 1800 poems (with fewer than a dozen published in her lifetime), followed by a popular, heavily edited posthumous 1890 collection, seem eerily to have set the stage for contentious critical discussion in the following century, of poems first normalized by commas into acceptable form.[1] Not until Thomas H. Johnson's 1955 scholarly edition were they at last restored into the restless, disturbing dashes that exploded from her pen. Even

[1]As Robert Weisbuch explains of the effect of her dashes, "Dickinson suddenly, midpoem, has her thought change, pulls in the reins on her faith, and introduces a realistic doubt; and we are right there as this occurs" (Weisbuch, "Prisming" 214). Earlier, he claimed: "Apparently then, the dashes work. How? They are a final, most iconic example of that merger between pure thought and individuated experience which we have traced throughout Dickinson's poetic strategy" (Weisbuch, *Poetry* 73).

then, the controversy did not subside; on the contrary, critical divisions about Dickinson's intentions and possibilities have grown ever more tendentious.

It is worth pausing here in the shift away from prose fiction to consider how the status of punctuation is altered by poetry's configuration in lines. After all, end-stopped lines confirm the weight of punctuational finality, while enjambed lines slide sense along by refusing to culminate at the line break. Indeed, enjambment allows line ends to serve as a form of silent punctuation unavailable to prose: more moderate than typographical marks; encouraging a quicker pace even as conflicting ideas are brought together. The particular poetic implications of dashes over commas, or of semicolons over periods, may differ little from their characteristic resonance in prose, though the additional weight of the line compounds their effects. And Dickinson forms a dramatic example to consider just such effects, even taking her poetic lines *as lines* more or less for granted. Consider Kamilla Denman's astute claim about her verse as at once musical and rhythmical:

> Dickinson's punctuation is neither a transcendent, purely extra-semantic effect nor a careless transgression of grammatical rules but an integral part of her exploration of language, used deliberately to disrupt conventional grammatical patterns and create new relationships between words; to resist stasis in linguistic expression (whether in the conventions of printing or in her own evolving writing); to create musical and rhythmical effects; and to affirm the silent and the nonverbal, the spaces between words that lend resonance and emphasis to poetry. (Denman 24)

That affirmation of the "spaces between words" reminds us how productively dashes spark vibrant interpretive possibilities not only in our reading of paragraphs and sentences (as James would later demonstrate for fiction) but also in smaller units (as Dickinson had already anticipated), exfoliating brief clauses and individual words into profoundly consequential segments of poetic meaning. The dashes that proliferate throughout, often at the ends of lines, are lent an additional, dramatic weight by virtue of their placement on the page.[2]

The link between punctuation and musical pauses has long configured poetical assessments, given prominence in Adorno's own strong interpretive gestures. Yet Dickinson raises the stakes in jewel-like lyrics that at once defy and enhance brief verbal gestures. Or as Denman adds, "Like songs set to music, Dickinson's poems are accompanied by a punctuation of varying pauses, tones, and rhythms that extend, modify, and emancipate her words, while pointing to the silent places from which language erupts" (Denman 24).[3] The effect of Dickinson's preferences becomes clear in her singular objection to the newspaper alteration of "The Snake." An energetic editor had altered capitalization, stanzas, even words themselves, though significantly Dickinson objected only to the repeated obliteration of her dashes. As Strunk and White remind us in their prescriptive standard guide, a dash is conventionally "stronger than a comma, less formal than a colon, and more relaxed than parentheses" (Strunk and White

[2]As Christanne Miller observes: "Dickinson gives no sign of being flexible about her style of punctuation. She lists alternative words in poems; she apologizes for her misspellings and modernizes archaisms in later copies of early poems; but she never apologizes for her unorthodox punctuation or provides variants for it" (Miller, *Grammar* 50).

[3]Somewhat more cautiously, Denman adds a valuable historical context for understanding the shift in editorial protocols:

It must be stressed that ideas about punctuation were by no means uniform in Dickinson's time. In the eighteenth and nineteenth centuries, there was a lively debate about pointing theory. The elocutionary school held that punctuation had a primarily rhetorical function: to indicate the length of pauses and rises and falls in the voice when declaiming a written piece. But as the medium of print became more widespread, the syntactic school gained increasing support, claiming that the primary function of punctuation was to reveal the grammatical structure of each sentence. In the absence of a voice to clarify ambiguities about the relations of words to one another, the eye must take the place of the ear in receiving and interpreting meaning. Park Honan tells us that by mid-century, the syntactical view had prevailed over the elocutionary. (Denman 23, fn. 4)

9). However "relaxed," the dash nonetheless seems abrupt and emphatic if paradoxically informal, making it perfect for Dickinson's own spectacularly paradoxical purposes.

This anxiety about editorial mangling reflects Dickinson's refusal to have her poems domesticated linguistically, their meanings transformed and subdued by conventional habits of punctual (and punctuational) decorum. And the measure of that increasing anxiety is the degree to which it is reflected in the evolution of her stylistic choices: "from conventional punctuation in the earliest poems through a prolific period where punctuation pulled apart every normal relationship of the parts of speech, to a time of grim redefinition punctuated by weighty periods, on to a final stage where language and punctuation are minimal but intensely powerful" (Denman 30).[4] As Denman further points out, even Dickinson's copying of earlier poems transformed punctuation to her later preference, and with newer poems investing dashes with an "anarchic" force by replacing "almost every other mark of punctuation and in its placement between almost every one of the parts of speech" (Denman 32).[5] The dash defies the sur-

---

[4]Denman observes the diminishing use of dashes in later Dickinson, and that they seem most prevalent in what she describes as the urgent period of 1862–63. For disagreement with this claim, see Sharon Cameron (and Denman's argument against her). Paul Crumbley observes that following Dickinson's resistance to religious conversion, dropping out of Mount Holyoke in 1849, "we see a steady increase in confidence along with a corresponding dependence on dashes" in her letters (Crumbley 75).

[5]Paul Crumbley explains "Dickinson's experiments with poetic voice. The broad category of marks that come under the heading 'dash' suggest subtle gradations of inflection and syntactic disjunction that multiply the voices in poems and letters" (Crumbley 1). Or as he later states, more strongly: "Rather than being a painful symbol of loss and division, the dash suggests that disjunction, to Dickinson, is one of the defining characteristics of the self in language" (Crumbley 15). Crumbley believes Dickinson's dashes can be subdivided semantically depending on length and angle:

> Our solution to the difficulty of matching print to Dickinson's variable "dashes" has been the creation of sixteen dash types, each of which stands for a range of similar handwritten marks. The end result is visual

prised closure proffered by exclamation marks, offering instead
the apparent continuity of a horizontal wrinkle; at times, it seems
a line connecting what would otherwise be the dots of ellipsis,
transfiguring possible silence into dashed fragments and broken
thoughts.[6] Indeed, dashes seem like an all but figurative break
from continuity, from syntax itself in its efforts to draw things
quietly, imperceptibly into grammatical coherence. "What is interesting," Susan Howe has observed of this effect, "is that she
found sense in the chance meeting of words. Forward progress
disrupted reversed. Sense came after suggestion" (Howe, *My* 24).
And that occurs precisely because meaning is signaled by punctuation.

> semblance rather than exact replication. We have, for instance, angled all
> the upward- and downward-slanting marks at 20 degrees, not because
> Dickinson's angles were uniform but because this angle fairly reflects the
> visual character of her multiple angles. To represent the different lengths
> of Dickinson marks, we developed six types that either extend or reduce
> the en-dash. (Crumbley u.p. preface).

Christanne Miller offers a salutary perspective: "Several critics have attempted to
categorize her 'pointing marks,' dividing her slanting lines into (among others)
angular slants, vertical slants, elongated periods, stress marks, and half-moon
marks, and differentiating them according to their position above, at, or below the
writing line. No one has argued convincingly, however, that such categorizations
in any appreciable way affect our reading of the poems" (Miller 50).

[6]Again, as Denman argues:

> Unlike the exclamation mark, the dash that dominates the prolific period
> is a horizontal stroke, on the level of this world. It both reaches out and
> holds at bay. Its origins in ellipsis connect it semantically to planets and
> cycles (rather than linear time and sequential grammatical progression),
> as well as to silence and the unexpressed. But to dash is also "to strike
> with violence so as to break into fragments; to drive impetuously forth
> or out, cause to rush together; to affect or qualify with an element of a
> different strain thrown into it; to destroy, ruin, confound, bring to nothing,
> frustrate, spoil; to put down on paper, throw off, or sketch, with hasty and
> unpremeditated vigour; to draw a pen vigorously through writing so as
> to erase it; [is] used as a euphemism for 'damn,' or as a kind of verbal
> imprecation; [or is] one of the two signals (the other being the dot) which
> in various combinations make up the letters of the Morse alphabet."
> (Denman 32–33)

The effect of Dickinson's dashes is evident nearly everywhere in her oeuvre, revealed in even such a less refractory effort as "Remorse—is Memory—awake" (1863) (Dickinson, *Poems* 383). For here, they appear as the only and ubiquitous form of punctuation, serving the reversal so central to the poem's logic:

> Remorse—is Memory—awake
> Her parties all astir—
> A Presence of Departed Acts—
> At window—and at Door—
>
> Its Past—set down before the Soul
> And lighted with a Match—
> Perusal—to facilitate—
> And help Belief to stretch—
>
> Remorse is cureless—the Disease
> Not even God—can heal—
> For 'tis His institution—and
> The Adequate of Hell—

One might initially overlook the wall-to-wall dashes as ancillary and unneeded, something like a punctuational spasm that seems irrelevant to the poem's meaning. Certainly, that appears true at first, with "Remorse—is Memory—awake / Her parties all astir." Yet we quickly realize that dashes effectively isolate single words, sequestering them off, sapping them of buttressing support or shored up meanings by their very posture of standing alone. As Sharon Cameron observes of the paradox inherent in the opening line (and compounded by its punctuation), it presents a definition that "exists for the purpose of dismissing the situation with which it purports to deal" (Cameron, *Lyric* 35).[7]

---

[7] Robert Weisbuch more generally asserts of Dickinson's paradoxical formulations: "These negations of vision create their own vision in turn: the symbolic intelligence which sees everlasting paradise in a commonplace pleasure must see death and hell in a commonplace pain. Thus, 'Remorse' becomes 'The Adequate of Hell—' (744) .... Dickinson does not proclaim and proselytize in this second

Yet that does not clarify why the line is enjambed, flowing without a dash into what seems like a new situation. For pausing here, one realizes that the announced identity ("Remorse—is Memory") enacts a more complicated entanglement, with regret over the past somehow transformed into a more spirited reconstruction *of* that past, and with the dash separating the nouns itself offering a reversal that functions not just temporally (turning us backward) but also emotionally forward (enlivening an otherwise quiescent and settled regret).[8] Memory is not simply alive here, but because *not* partitioned off by punctuation is thereby conceived as signally energized by all her inflamed parts.

Still, the restlessness of this feeling emerges in the next line via the transformation of "parties all astir" into a series of already "Departed Acts," conjoined sonically in the repetition that aligns

world; she confesses" (Weisbuch, *Poetry* 2). Offering an enacted interpretation, Sharon Leiter claims:

> By personifying Remorse and Memory and the Presence of Departed Acts, the poet creates the drama of a startling and painful awakening in the middle of the night. Instead of being told that the speaker's own sleep has been disturbed, we are given an image, parallel to and probably motivated by that disturbance. Memory, which has been sleeping, is jarred by the arrival of unexpected visitors at window and door. The "Parties all astir—" in this house of the soul may be merely "interested parties" or, as Dickinson's dictionary records, "disputants" on "opposite sides" of an issue. The agitation and inner conflict stirred by the sudden arrival, as well as a sense of immediacy, are enhanced by the use of dashes, in place of a connecting verb ("Her Parties *are* all astir *as they see* 'A Presence of Departed Acts—'"). Of course, the lack of logical connection also leaves open the possibility that the disputing parties *are* the departed acts themselves. Instead of a neat, one-to-one correspondence between images and what they represent, Dickinson achieves a sense of upheaval and disorientation. (Leiter 167–68)

[8] As Cameron continues: "Remorse (for that is the match) illuminates the past so that the flash revealed to us is simply accusatory. . . . The hell of remorse is that it blinds us to the real meanings of our experiences and simultaneously convinces us that the distortion we are seeing in place of that meaning is reality" (Cameron, *Lyric* 36).

physical aspects with memorable moments. It is as if the reversals endorsed (indeed enforced) by the punctuation lay at the poem's thematic center itself, in the about-face of feeling and remembrance, of synecdochic part and whole, of "Acts" that though "Departed" remain nonetheless an imperative "Presence." And their imputed presence peers presumably out through the "window" of memory even as it accompanies us through the "Door" of the past.

Remorse deliberately invokes "Its Past—set down" in the second quatrain, in wanting to examine what led to the present sense of contrition, pressing against consciousness so as finally to be explained and somehow resolved. Again, the dash dramatizes the temporal dissonance of a past refusing to stay passed, being deliberately exposed to the flame of possible insight. But the pun of "a Match" also doubles in the effort to match present remorse with past facts, bringing an alignment between them across the bridge created by the dash. And the sequence of three quick dashes to separate four words confirms the hesitancy, the possible misgiving, the hemming and hawing involved in the Soul's facing up to the body's history.

Only in the third quatrain, which erases the hesitancy of the poem's opening line with a simple un-dashed claim that "Remorse is cureless," do we realize that Belief cannot be stretched so far as to erase our guilt at the life we have actually lived. It is a Disease that accompanies our fallen state, with even God's saving grace unable to heal, as the isolating dashes again reveal. Remorse becomes "His institution," the everyday reminder of our daily fall, our recurrent inadequacy to separate past insufficiency from present aspiration, memory from regret. There is no faultless state that renders us whole or feeling at one with ourselves, able to move beyond contrition to some simpler, unified consciousness. And that realization of our partial, self-divided state is configured no more effectively than in the recurrent, ubiquitous dashes that structure the poem with their disruptive, cleaving effect (visually, grammatically, sonically).

What begins as a seemingly simple set of individual words set apart, apparently consisting of standalone lexical meanings—much like the regrettable separate acts that often punctuate our lives—is transformed through the course of the poem into an integrated if ever conflicting sequence of possibilities pitched against one another.[9] In that regard, "Remorse—is Memory—awake" offers a perfect example of Dickinson's signature consciousness, one that so often begins by focusing on single words, only to unfold their linked resonances and paradoxical conflicts in a larger epistemological, often theological frame of reference. At this point, however, one can well appreciate how much was lost in the altering by generations of editors of her punctuation, from breathtaking dashes to workaday commas. It is also worth considering briefly (from another perspective) the ways in which Dickinson's intense devotion to the logic of dashes distinguishes her vision from, say, Faulkner's parenthetical constructions and comma-loaded (even comma-spliced) sentences, which depend not on reversals of logic so much as self-embedding connections.

Dickinson's dashes, however, hardly work the same way in different poems, any more than Faulkner's parentheses or Baldwin's commas or James's dashes do in different narratives (and sometimes even the same ones). Signature punctuation marks may appear "signature" as part of a writer's larger unified style, but separate instances among that same writer's stories, novels, and poems put pressure on punctuation differently, producing effects that idiosyncratically alter our readings anew. The deeply necessary

[9]For a further interpretive angle, see Sharon Cameron's reading based upon Dickinson's fascicle groupings: "To see a poem contextualized by a fascicle is sometimes to see that it has an altogether different, rather than only a relationally more complex, meaning when it is read in sequence rather than as an isolated lyric" (Cameron, "Dickinson's Fascicles" 149). In response to Cameron's urging to read the poems contextually, one might observe that "Remorse—is Memory—awake" appears in the middle of fascicle 37, between "The Birds reported from the South—" (a poem ostensibly about forgetting spring's allures) and "Renunciation—is a piercing Virtue—" (about "letting go")—both of which do provide an interpretive context for the poem.

conflict produced by the dashes that structure "Remorse—is Memory—awake" (J744) becomes in a slightly later effort a more calibrated, even fanciful gesture. "One and One—are One—" (Dickinson, *Poems* J769) appears from its opening mathematical axiom to be less a reflection on recondite emotional plangencies than a whimsical brain teaser:

> One and One—are One—
> Two—be finished using—
> Well enough for Schools—
> But for Minor Choosing—
>
> Life—just—or Death—
> Or the Everlasting—
> More—would be too vast
> For the Soul's Comprising—

As always, Dickinson challenges the reader to pursue elliptical declarations, with the opening line recalling the *Phaedo*, in which Socrates explores why the unity of body and soul should become the problem of how one independent body plus one separate soul can still exist as "One." That helps explain the plural copula "are," in a slight tilt away from conventional expression "is," if only to affirm a wondrous convergence rather than mere addition. Then following a second dash, more period than pause, "One" is agreed to replace the conventional "Two," which becomes a simple-minded arithmetic solution to a sublunary problem ("for Minor Choosing"). The reference of "Well enough for Schools" suggestively invokes a scholasticism that strives for dialectical reasoning as a means of resolving contradictions. But the opening challenge holds to a paradox that cannot be so reasonably resolved.[10]

Not until the second quatrain (of a poem built on "One" and "Two") does an adequate explanation appear, though it sustains the initial paradox via a hesitancy established through its half-dozen

---

[10]The poem occurs, to contextualize again, in Fascicle 23 between "The Beggar Lad—dies early" and "I lived on Dread—." Neither one on first reading seems useful in understanding the mid-sequence poem. See Miller 247.

destabilizing dashes. The customary division of life and death is defied by a third term ("Everlasting"), revealing that binary systems cannot account for such overarching considerations, working only as a matter of "Minor Choosing." The collapse of "Life— just" with its own contrary "Death" becomes a cause of revelation in which "the Everlasting— / More—") exceeds any common actuarial balancing we might achieve. The poem finally depends on earthly mathematics it nonetheless rejects unhesitatingly without a dash ("too vast / For the Soul's Comprising"), having banked on a binary equation inadequate to the realm revealed in the final "More—." If the earlier poem invoked dashes as a means of emotional pummeling at our ever-divided state, this forgoes emotion altogether, relying on dashes to make us pause over a logic that remains insufficient. In either case, however, Dickinson turns the dash to her own structuring ends, creating a complex vision that requires little other punctuation.[11]

---

[11]Paul Crumbley declares that "Close attention to the expanding life of words within the poems means reading with an eye toward spatial rather than linear progression. The dash liberates meaning from a syntax that would ordinarily narrow the field of reference for specific words; at the same time it alerts readers to the role they play in expanding these fields of reference" (Crumbley 29). Earlier, Geoffrey Hartman concluded of Dickinson's poetry: "Her attitude is almost spectatorial. Can we define that attitude exactly? It is clear that Emily Dickinson's art creates a space. It allows the threshold to exist; it extends the liminal moment" (Hartman 350). As he added, "Emily Dickinson does not 'tell all'; there is no staring recognition in her poetry. Her fate is to stay profane, outside the gates, though in sight of 'the promised end'" (Hartman 351). And that explains her infrequent periods, as Christanne Miller explains: "Dickinson is apt to use the period ironically, to mock the expectation of final certainty" (Miller, *Grammar* 53).

5
Expansion: Woolf's Semicolons

Buffeted by Dickinson's destabilizing dashes and in search of relief (as if guided by a dash), one would be hard-pressed to come up with an author less attuned to such slashes of meaning than Virginia Woolf (though Gustave Flaubert and William James make compelling candidates).[1] Her habitual use of "the semicolon, that supremely self-possessed valet of phraseology" (Baker 70) seems defiantly to jettison Hemingway's full stops and Henry

---

[1]Flaubert's delight in semicolons has long been noted, beginning with Marcel Proust's claim that he typically omits "and" for the last item in a list (such as three adjectives), but that he includes a colon or semicolon followed by "and" as "an indication that another part of the description is beginning, that the withdrawing wave is going once again to reform. . . . In short, 'and' in Flaubert always opens a minor clause and hardly ever concludes an enumeration" (Proust 591). Nabokov would later comment that "This *semicolon-and* comes after an enumeration of actions or states or objects, then the semicolon creates a pause and the *and* proceeds to round up the paragraph, to introduce a culminating image, or a vivid detail, descriptive, poetic, melancholy, or amusing. This is a peculiar feature of Flaubert's style" (Nabokov, *Lec* 171). For a wry survey of contemporary French proponents of the point-virgule (who argue that "the beauty of the semicolon, and its glory, lies in the support lent by this particular punctuation mark to the expression of a complex thought"), see Jon Henley.

Of William James, Ben Dolnick has stated:

> James's paragraphs, as lucid and unpretentious as can be, are divided and subdivided, as intricately structured as the anatomical diagrams he includes in "Psychology: Briefer Course." Semicolons, along with exclamation points and dashes and whole sackfuls of commas, are, for him, vital tools in keeping what he called the "stream of thought" from appearing to the reader as a wild torrent (Dolnick).

James's and Dickinson's reversible maneuvers in favor of sliding things along, doing so more decidedly than commas.[2] Outside of the compressed syllabic gymnastics of poetry, one might suppose this preference is linked somehow to gender dynamics, of intrepid (purportedly masculine) assurance in the power of sheer syntactical brevity or abrupt thematic about-faces versus more temperate feminine inflections that build cumulatively. But that is clearly too facile.

Consider *Mrs. Dalloway* (1925), in its gradual slippage from exclamation marks to commas, settling at last with a decided preference for semicolons. Part of the distinctive effect Woolf achieves is via sentences that never quite finish but linger instead protractedly, extending into byways, modifying themselves ever further, in the process accommodating an unfurling mode of contemplation. Ben Dolnick insists that semicolons uniquely honor "this movement of mind, this tendency of thoughts to proliferate like yeast"; and as if with Woolf in mind, he confirms: "No other piece of punctuation so compactly captures the way in which our thoughts are both liquid and solid, wave and particle" (Dolnick). In consort with this syntactic pattern, *Mrs. Dalloway* resists dividing into conventional sections, either chapters or "books," tending instead to advance amid swerves and diversions, interrupted only occasionally by breaks of white space.

That propulsive rhythm is largely generated by punctuation once again, even in the briefest of moments. Midway through the novel, Richard Dalloway makes a gift of roses to his wife out of a gesture of heartfelt love, appreciated from his perspective: "She

---

[2] According to Joseph Boone, Woolf uses parentheses in *Mrs. Dalloway* as a means of segregating social and emotional issues: "the quotidian detail, the social fabric, of daily life that one might expect of a society-oriented novel is continually deemphasized, often cordoned off in parentheses, while Clarissa's expansive memories deluge the foreground and provide the novel with its primary tension and interest" (Boone 178). More generally, Jennifer Brody claims: "These days the semicolon, one of the least loved, least understood marks, barely ekes out a living between the period and the comma. It suffers nightmares from its precarious situation" (Brody 141). See also Anna Davies 14; and Cecelia Watson, *passim*.

understood; she understood without his speaking; his Clarissa"
(Woolf 115). However straightforward and inconsequential the
moment may seem, the doubled semicolons achieve an oddly intense complication, as if Richard's emotion were transposed into
a wave of affection that laps against the shore of "his Clarissa."
And as with James's clotting of dashes in "Daisy Miller," a certain
clotting of semicolons occurs here, drawing attention to themselves.

Or take an earlier passage, triggered by Clarissa's apparent
regret—"Oh if she could have had her life over again!" (Woolf
10)—followed by thoughts of what "would have been," supplanted
in turn by her recurrent sense of immense dissatisfaction.

> But often now this body she wore (she stopped to look at a
> Dutch picture), this body, with all its capacities, seemed noth-
> ing—nothing at all. She had the oddest sense of being herself
> invisible; unseen; unknown; there being no more marrying,
> no more having of children now, but only this astonishing and
> rather solemn progress with the rest of them, up Bond Street,
> this being Mrs. Dalloway; not even Clarissa any more; this be-
> ing Mrs. Richard Dalloway. (Woolf 10)

Notice how the opening sentence, prompted by exclamatory
regret over the past, tumbles into a discombobulated flurry of
repetitions ("this body," "nothing") marked by commas, a parenthesis, and finally a dismal em dash reiteration. Yet Clarissa
quickly recovers control even in the midst of dismay; as the next
sentence flows back into consciousness, single words pause at the
behest of semicolons, then commas, then semicolons again. The
rhythm here seems notably varied, shifting mercurially as Clarissa's thoughts and feelings waver, with possibilities closed off by
a dash ("—nothing at all.") that then founders on a period, before
continuing with the dull beat of negations that constitute her present sense of herself.

And the semicolons calmly serve to confirm that negation, at
least as she perceives her state, building on each other not as abbreviated sentences (with firm full stops) or accumulating clauses

slightly slackened (through dilatory commas), but in a more per-
cussive beat that separately marks each clause, forcing the reader
to slow down and absorb one by one a series of distinct sovereign
judgments.[3] The next sentence extends the cadence, though shifting perspective from morose self-regard to a newly engaged delight with the world passing by:

> Bond Street fascinated her; Bond Street early in the morning
> in the season; its flags flying; its shops; no splash; no glitter;
> one roll of tweed in the shop where her father had bought his
> suits for fifty years; a few pearls; salmon on an iceblock.

> "That is all," she said, looking at the fishmonger's. "That is all,"
> she repeated, pausing for a moment. (Woolf 10–11)

What we quickly realize is not that Clarissa is inherently different
from a character in James, say, or even Hemingway, but that
Woolf's punctuational presentation of her reveals a consciousness
radically unlike any they attempt to imagine.

The resilient, spirited, wayward mode of thought by which
Clarissa shifts abruptly from discouragement to delight, from dis-
illusioned vision of her past suddenly interrupted by enchanted
glimpses of the present, seems characteristic of Woolf's creation.
It is as if each surveyed observation were isolated, held up to the

---

[3] Again, Joseph Boone observes:

> On the level of the sentence, Woolf creates highly elliptical structures that
> can easily cover the space of a page or more, structures whose phrases
> and clauses, sutured by semicolons that allow an unbroken accretion or
> amplification of detail within the individual sentence, force the reader
> to keep reading forward. Similarly, the ubiquitous use of present-tense
> participial phrases generates forward motion; their litanic repetition
> creates the sensation of action about to be completed, of meaning about to
> emerge, if we just keep pushing ahead. Complementing the strategic use
> of commas, semicolons, and dashes to extend such clauses and phrases
> in what come to seem endless, unbroken lines, Woolf frequently uses
> parentheses to open up spaces within the sentence or paragraph whose
> content creates a simultaneity of action or laying of multiple viewpoints
> without breaking the grammatical unit. (Boone 179)

light—an aperçu, an impressionist moment at once detached and woven into subjectivity. Woolf adapts the semicolon in strictly ungrammatical ways to detach the elliptical absolute construction more completely than otherwise from a continuous syntactic embrace.

The implications of this presentational method can perhaps best be ascertained by contrast with James's treatment of Marcher in *The Beast in the Jungle*, which begins: "The escape would have been to love her; then, *then* he would have lived." Despite the initial semicolon, thereafter punctuation appropriately serves to sideline and defer revelation of meaning, which is of course the story's premise. For Woolf, however, revelation occurs gradually, incrementally, parsed semicolon by semicolon, which also paradoxically enough occurs in large swatches of James (except for when it doesn't). These are moments when he, like she, homes in via hyper-punctuated sentences on a distinct idea or meaning.[4]

Yet it is not only Clarissa whose thoughts are mapped so, as we realize a few pages later in the shift to Lucrezia Smith, embarrassed by her husband Septimus's outburst in public: "People must notice; people must see. People, she thought, looking at the crowd staring at the motor car; the English people, with their children and their horses and their clothes, which she admired in a way; but they were 'people' now, because Septimus had said, 'I will kill myself'; an awful thing to say" (Woolf 15). Again, quickly as semicolons appear, they vanish, as Lucrezia teeters between absolute dismay and fond memories of the autumn before, mortified at how she appears to others, ironically matching Clarissa's self-consciousness about her own social status. Of course, even delight is expressed with similar punctuation, as Clarissa soon recalls her love of Sally Seton:

Then came the most exquisite moment of her whole life passing a stone urn with flowers in it. Sally stopped; picked a flower;

---

[4]Franco Moretti contrasts Woolf's focus with Joyce's style in *Ulysses* (1922), which he argues presents everything as an unfocused foreground (Moretti 156).

kissed her on the lips. The whole world might have turned up-side down! The others disappeared; there she was alone with Sally. And she felt that she had been given a present, wrapped up, and told just to keep it, not to look at it—a diamond. (Woolf 35)

The sequence from run-on summation, to recollection broken into triple semicoloned clauses, to a compound sentence express-ing the rapture Clarissa feels about the gift of love: it is as if Woolf engineers her prose to capture the intersection of present ebul-lient emotion and past transforming event.

Granted, periods do seem to reinforce closure, sealing off uncertainty that can emerge with semicolons: "She was not old yet. She had just broken into her fifty-second year. Months and months of it were still untouched" (Woolf 36). But semicolons unfold and blossom into a certain psychological reassurance, as when Peter tries to grasp Clarissa's allure through a series of ne-gations that suddenly become a simple affirmation, repeated for emphasis: "Not that she was striking; not beautiful at all; there was nothing picturesque about her; she never said anything spe-cially clever; there she was, however; there she was" (Woolf 74). And the very proliferation of semicolons here at once anticipates and enforces the thought's very constancy, persevering at last as the closing lines of the novel itself.

No syntactical rule applies absolutely, of course, and the ef-fect of different forms of punctuation alters through the novel. But Clarissa's lively openness to incompatible possibilities se-questered by semicolons does contrast rhythmically with those who never swerve from sanguine beliefs. And that unflappable self-confidence achieves its own cadence in the augmented syn-tax calmly endorsed by commas, with accretions and additions brooking less hesitation than extending confirmation. Consider the close-minded vision of Sir William Bradshaw, expressed as an unquestioning faith: "Shredding and slicing, dividing and subdi-viding, the clocks of Harley Street nibbled at the June day, coun-seled submission, upheld authority, and pointed out in chorus the supreme advantages of a sense of proportion" (Woolf 100). The clauses simply ratify the proportionate logic of "shredding and slicing," as if a mechanical series of subdivisions were converted through the magic of syntactic apposition into a common good.

Tellingly, Bradshaw's unblinkered trust in convention is matched by unshakeable others, as Clarissa considers Miss Kilman's ruthless efforts to convert her daughter Elizabeth, just before she contemplates the alternative in an attentive (yet tentative) view of her elderly neighbor:

> The cruelest things in the world, she thought, seeing them clumsy, hot, domineering, hypocritical, eavesdropping, jealous, infinitely cruel and unscrupulous, dressed in a mackintosh coat, on the landing; love and religion. Had she ever tried to convert any one herself? Did she not wish everybody merely to be themselves? And she watched out of the window the old lady opposite climbing upstairs. Let her climb upstairs if she wanted to; let her stop; then let her, as Clarissa had often seen her, gain her bedroom, part her curtains, and disappear again into the background. (Woolf 123)

In the punctuation itself we are confirmed in twin halves of this passage, revealing two possibilities for facing life: one, in comma-burdened arrogance; the other, in diffident openhandedness. Clarissa's delight in "the privacy of the soul" (Woolf 123) finds confirmation in the syntax of her expression, as she refuses the beguiling balm of "love and religion" involved in wanting to change another.[5] The mindful, even apparently "legal" semicolons dividing clauses in the last sentence are kindly intended to allow the old woman her temporal autonomy. What we realize about Clarissa is that the visual marking itself of her expressions

---

[5]And not only Clarissa. Richard's own self-division between certitude and surprise is likewise conveyed through differently noted pauses: "It was a miracle. Here he was walking across London to say to Clarissa in so many words that he loved her. Which one never does say, he thought. Partly one's lazy; partly one's shy. And Clarissa—it was difficult to think of her; except in starts, as at luncheon when he saw her quite distinctly; their whole life" (Woolf 112). And the rest of his thoughts continue to stress his hesitations.

becomes a rendering of consciousness, already revealing her flex-ible, ever inquiring, open-minded view of life in London.

Again, it is worth noting that Woolf's preference in *Mrs. Dal-loway* for the accretive possibilities of semicolons does not extend as fully to her other, later works. With Hemingway, the terse style of abrupt period-ending sentences worked effectively to realize the vision of his early stories, though his novels tended to modu-late into a less clipped, more expansive style. James, by contrast, incorporated dashes as an essential structuring component of his signature perspective, early and late, in both published fictional and private epistolary realms. Critics of Dickinson have as-tutely identified a particular biographical period where she in-dulged a predilection for dashes, invoking them more often than she had earlier or later. In Woolf's first masterpiece, we are aware of a writer not simply discovering the possibilities of punctua-tion but inventing a distinctive style adequate to her characters' various (and only gradually revealed) capacities. By *To the Light-house* (1927), two years later, she would alter strategies further in sentences that skip and dance, weaving clauses together through runs of commas; in fact, eleven of them on the first page divide up a hundred-word sentence, and rarely do two simple sentences (two periods) occur in sequence. Indeed, here and after she pep-pers her prose with semicolons, dashes, parentheses, exclamation marks, and ellipses.

As if to extend the possibilities of the semicolon, Andre Du-bus II offers a very different rendition of consciousness in a story that models its syntax after Woolf's characteristic mode. Only six pages long, "A Love Song" divides into distinct (white-space-divided) paragraphs, with some twenty-nine semicolons clus-tered at particular moments (in the fifth, twelfth, and fourteenth paragraphs)—clustering that reminds us of James's own fusing of punctuation in "Daisy Miller." Here, however, the recurrent punc-tuation registers the devastated consciousness of a wife named Catherine abandoned by her unnamed husband. Consider the fifth paragraph, pinballing among fifteen commas, a couple of colons thrown in, with five interruptive semicolons breaking up the closing cadences of this long single sentence:

> She never again perceived time as she had before, as a child, then an adolescent: a graceful and merry and brown-haired girl, in infinite preparation, infinite waiting, for love; and as a woman loved and in love: with peaceful and absolute hope gestating daughters, and bravely, even for minutes gratefully, enduring the pain of their births; a woman who loved daughters and a man, would bear her daughters' sorrow and pain for them if she could, would give up her life to keep theirs; and loved him with a passion whose deeper and quicker current through the years delighted her; gave at times a light to her eyes, a hue of rose to her cheeks; loved him, too, with the sudden and roiling passion of consolable wrath; and with daily and nightly calm, the faithful certainty that was the river she became until it expelled her to dry on its bank. (Dubus 22)

The entire emotional arc of the story is contained in this run-on single-sentence biography of "before," not simply with the tumultuous repetitions of "love" and its denial but with its variously timed hesitations. And hesitations marked out so differently.

The question, however, lies in what ways the semicolons and colons differ from commas in their overall effect. Do they actually offer a meaningfully fuller pause, and if so, why? Can the clauses be interpreted idiosyncratically based on their different punctuation? Of course, in both instances the answer is "yes," though leading in separate turns to separable interpretations.[6] In either

---

[6]According to Ernesto Franco, "what is juxtaposed" by the semicolon "is both separated and united"; the semicolon requires the reader to interpret because "'the interpretation of the semicolon is not simple but open' it is 'a mark that raises doubts'" (cited by Dury xlviii).

Among notable writers, Robert Louis Stevenson offers (like Dubus) a strong contrast to Woolf in his "obsession" with semicolons. Richard Dury, for instance, claims that he relies on its "frequent use" for "fragmentation" (Dury, "Introduction" xlvii), and that he "typically places a semicolon before a

of dual cases, however, this paragraph is followed by others in which the frequency of colons diminishes sharply before Catherine takes "her first lover," and suddenly the unpredictable emotional turmoil seems reflected in another paragraph of mixed, volatile punctuation. When that relation ends, she meets a divorcée whose anguish over his marital betrayals matches her own:

> She learned all of this while drinking two Manhattans at the party; then she went home with him, to his apartment without plants or flowers or feminine scents, a place that seemed without light, though its windows were tall and broad; then she knew why: it was not a place where someone lived; he ate

conjunction, perhaps to render problematic the link between the two parts of the sentence" (Dury "Stevenson"). Barry Menikoff offers an analysis of Stevenson's punctuation as "integral" to his "main objective of replicating the Pacific world that he knew so well" (Menikoff 35). Not only his "calculated and deliberate" use of commas, or his "unsettling" syntax (Menikoff 38), but his quarrels with compositors who altered his manuscripts reveal that concern.

> But the semicolon is the triggering device, revealing Stevenson's habit of stringing together details in a loosely punctuated sequence. Through the lucidity of his prose Stevenson discloses a fundamental irony: that things in the world are not clear and lucid; that the more one aspires to express their coherence, and is successful at it, the more one recognizes the futility of the pursuit; that language itself, and the way in which we organize and build our sentences, provide an illusion at odds with reality. The semicolon, with its pause—virtually a full stop, yet not the end of a sentence—fits Stevenson's scheme beautifully: it is neither a terminal mark, like a period, nor an intermediate device, like a comma. This ambiguity is apparent even in simple compound sentences, where Stevenson almost invariably uses the semicolon. He does not separate the clauses with periods, nor does he use commas. It is as if he were not sure whether to make his statements independent or to connect them. There is an uncertainty built into his style that is encouraged or assisted by his use of the semicolon. (Menikoff 43)

Even earlier, Graham Good observed of Stevenson: "In sentence structure, he liked to produce a kind of 'knot' or 'hitch,' a 'moment of suspended meaning' (this may account for his near-addictive use of the semi-colon). The aim is to create suspense on the syntactical as well as the plot level" (Good 51; see as well Dupee, "Stevenson").

and slept there and did this in his double bed, did this tenderly,
wickedly; his home was like an ill-kept motel. (Dubus 25–26)

The impersonality of his apartment matches the single sentence's
own disarray: with its stream of consciousness paused by a
semicolon; then a series of less interruptive commas; then a
semicolon again; before finally being put on full pause with a
colon that announces this was not "a place where someone lived."
The very confusion, intensely felt, in Catherine's discovery of the
man she thinks she knows is reflected in the paragraph's hiccuping punctuation.

For a writer so attuned to swings of emotional perturbation,
it seems odd that Dubus does not evoke those states more often through such punctuational shuffling. But here, with our eyes
scanning the page as if over a far-off landscape, emotions are silently swayed by a topography we barely notice *as* topography.[7]
Again, as with Woolf, the punctuated rhythm of the narrative not
simply mirrors the affair but actively creates its rhythm, of en-
gagement yet reserve, of tenderness yet self-division. What seems
at moments like an indefinite continuation becomes at others a
chronicle of sudden, abrupt pauses shackled by doubt, as if the
sexual allure that had finally engaged Catherine and seemed to
give her peace were altered by punctuation itself, the unstated
turns in a sentence and a relationship that reveal how impossible
the two (sentences, relationships) actually turn out to be.

Dubus's smooth punctuational shaping offers a sharp contrast
to other American authors, equally notable. Willa Cather, for instance, has a well-deserved reputation for lyricism, though she

---

[7]Russell Bogue has observed a completely different context of "the word
'topography' applied to language: Mandarin Chinese. Tonal languages (like
Mandarin, Cantonese, and Vietnamese) are often said to have an auditory
topography. To romanize Chinese requires using accents that graphically represent
what one's voice must do while pronouncing the syllable. Thus, the sentence
wo hĕn xíhūan shūo zhōngwén ('I like to speak Chinese') physically instantiates
what you will hear when someone is conveying this meaning to you. Attention
to the aural topography of the sentence is a key part of Chinese poetry" (private
communication).

generally achieves that effect with only a minimal play of punctuation, tending to echo or otherwise simply elaborate expressions otherwise stated straightforwardly. Rarely does she deviate from a conventional syntactical structure, exemplified in Tom Outland's account in *The Professor's House* (1925):

> The bluish rock and the sun-tanned grass, under the unusual purple-grey of the sky, gave the whole valley a very soft colour, lavender and pale gold, so that the occasional cedars growing beside the borders looked black that morning. It may have been the hint of snow in the air, but it seemed to me that I had never breathed in anything that tasted so pure as the air in that valley. (Cather 178)

The passage is punctuated as it is because her syntax demands almost no punctuation at all; nothing is "left out" and therefore nothing needs to be added, grammatically speaking. Indeed, we might remove even the few marks she does insert without altering either rhythm or sense, perhaps because the limpid revelations of prose stripped to such colorful description is enough, without the entangling pauses and brakings registered by interruptive signs.[8] Cormac McCarthy likewise tends to avoid unusual punctuation, as shown in Adam Calhoun's "heat map" of *Blood Meridian*, revealing merely that he depends on question marks as an indication of his reliance on *how* dialogue is presented and subsequently referred to. In fact, the most common punctuation in McCarthy are periods, followed by commas, confirming again how thoroughly McCarthy was, even early in his career, a stalwart of Hemingway rather than Faulkner, at least syntactically speaking.

---

[8]As Janet Giltrow and David Stouck observe, "The echo effect, that reverberation of something from the past, is one of the most obvious and accessible of Cather's literary techniques. Traditionally, critics have approached it through studies of repetition and parallelism" (Giltrow and Stouck 11).

6
Hemorrhage: Joyce, Morrison, Saramago, Sebald

At this point, it may be worth addressing more forcibly what punctuation achieves by turning to passages that abandon its sway altogether. For without marks to stem the ongoing verbal stream, run-on prose tends to produce a hemorrhaging effect, as if the figurative tourniquet of periods and commas no longer tightened and compressed lexical choices into viable form. That effect can be offset by the systole and diastole of syntactical word order, but with no punctuation at all we are left with a more or less unimpeded flow of surging, turbulent lexemes. Still, by contrast with writers above who sometimes seem to indulge too exaggerated a taste for punctuation, others have inventively experimented with the opposite. And the absence of marks in their work reveals possibilities—cadenced, rhythmic, even musical—that are not discerned so dramatically in conventionally marked prose. Simply taking out periods and dashes, even serial commas, opens up intriguing ambiguities and semantic opportunities that can enrich our reading, if at the seemingly unwelcome price of slowing us down. Keep in mind that the long history of punctuation since the first millennium CE has been one of increasing attention to ever-expanding punctuational maneuvers. The more recent turn to a punctuation-less terrain all too familiar to early scribes thus offers an intriguing reminder of how prose was actually first meant to be read.

One possibly perverse way to engage the issue is by reversing the punctuational habit of even a minimalist like Hemingway, removing the reliable periods he felt it necessary to invoke at the very least. But did he genuinely need them for semantic clarity or could syntax have done the work by itself? As importantly, does the accented rhythm of his signature early style remain roughly the same without such nominal marks? The answers may not be altogether forthcoming, though a vignette from *In Our Time* offers something like a test for how linked (or alternatively, disconnected) punctuation can seem from syntax:

> *It was a frightfully hot day. We'd jammed an absolutely perfect barricade across the bridge. It was simply priceless. A big old wrought-iron grating from the front of a house. Too heavy to lift and you could shoot through it and they would have to climb over it. It was absolutely topping. They tried to get over it, and we potted them from forty yards. They rushed it, and officers came out along and worked on it. It was an absolutely perfect obstacle. Their officers were very fine. We were frightfully put out when we heard the flank had gone, and we had to fall back.*
> (Hemingway 37)

In pausing over the pulse and tempo here, we begin to suspect that the passage may not need punctuation at all, at least to achieve its fragmented effect. Quite the contrary:

> *It was a frightfully hot day we'd jammed an absolutely perfect barricade across the bridge it was simply priceless a big old wrought-iron grating from the front of a house too heavy to lift and you could shoot through it and they would have to climb over it it was absolutely topping they tried to get over it and we potted them from forty yards they rushed it and officers came out along and worked on it it was an absolutely perfect obstacle their officers were very fine we were frightfully put out when we heard the flank had gone and we had to fall back.*

It is as if Hemingway's modulated verbal expression were enough, unmarked, since even his minimal full stops simply coordinate discriminations and elaborations that straightforward syntax already lays out.

Among the first to anticipate this realization was James Joyce, whose closing eighteenth section to *Ulysses* offers in Molly Bloom's long soliloquy a narrative all but entirely lacking in marks at all. Though it consists of eight apparent run-on "sentences," they are defined not by periods but by paragraphing: the only punctuational device allowed. Beginning innocuously, the section moves via conjunctions, prepositions, and restrictive clauses:

> Yes because he never did a thing like that before as ask to get his breakfast in bed with a couple of eggs since the *City Arms* hotel when he used to be pretending to be laid up with a sick voice doing his highness to make himself interesting to that old faggot Mrs Riordan that he thought he had a great leg of and she never left us a farthing all for masses for herself and her soul greatest miser ever was actually afraid to lay out 4d for her methylated spirit telling me all her ailments she had too much old chat in her about politics and earthquakes and the end of the world let us have a bit of fun first. (Joyce 997)

Flowing from an initially affirmative "Yes," Molly's stream of consciousness quickly shifts to annoyance at being asked to serve her husband breakfast in bed, finally to a culminating orgasmic shiver pages later as she recalls his marriage proposal years before, concluding her uninterrupted monologue:

> and Gibraltar as a girl where I was a Flower of the mountain yes when I put the rose in my hair like the Andalusian girls used or shall I wear a red yes and how he kissed me under the Moorish wall and I thought well as well him as another and then I asked him with my eyes to ask again yes and then he asked me would I yes to say yes my mountain flower and first I put my arms around him yes and drew him down to me so he could feel my breasts all perfume yes and his heart was going like mad and yes I said yes I will Yes. (Joyce 1069)

Even here, the capitalizations of the passage seem superfluous, the final period extraneous, while polysyndeton throughout renders clauses clearly understood, as if something of an invisible line break that poetically serves as faux punctuation.

Each of the long monologue's eight unpunctuated sections seems to operate as a sentence, in part because of syntactical conventions that allow readers to intuit where sentence divisions *would* in fact be (though neither Molly Bloom nor Joyce decides to enforce those divisions). That creates an interesting tension between the reader's impulse toward structure and the novel's defiance of it, at least here, with a conspicuous lack of discriminating marks. And in part *because* unpunctuated, the final section enforces a narrative and emotional return, circling back on itself in far from random sequence. Indeed, modeled on Homer's *Odyssey*, the entire novel traces a circular cycle, with Molly's monologue (the only female voice in *Ulysses*) returning at last to its opening affirmation. Marking a forward and backward weaving of words, she matches Penelope's ancient weaving and unweaving of the burial shroud meant to deter beleaguering suitors. Moreover, that warp and weft tension, alternately created and released, prominently occurs at the lexical level, as Lisa Sternlieb observes:

> Leaving out any direct reference to weaving, while the rest of the novel is rife with such allusions, Molly instead plays with a wide range of related words. By omitting apostrophes she puns with several words crucial to her narrative—"cant," "wed," "ill," "wont," and especially "weve." In a passage which clearly illustrates her ability to weave and unweave simultaneously, she shows how women are deserving of contempt and pity: "weve none either he wants what he wont get or its some woman ready to stick her knife in you I hate that in women no wonder they treat us the way they do we are a dreadful lot of bitches I suppose its all the troubles we have makes us so snappy Im not like that." Contradictions are seamlessly woven into Molly's pattern as she moves from "weve none" to "all the troubles we have." (Sternlieb 110)

Displaying a capacious ability to balance these contradictions, Molly gradually fashions meaning out of what seems initially formless.

More generally and at the level of syntax, we slowly realize how fully the absence of punctuation throughout this final section reveals the most elaborate structure of the novel. The whole is tightly organized according to an octagonal pattern, Diane Tolomeo argues, with sentences paired forward and backward leading to a rich fabric of consciousness: "as Molly relaxes and begins to sink into the misty realm which precedes sleep, her thoughts become richer and more inclusive: a withdrawal from and an embracing of the world appear as two aspects of the same process" (Tolomeo 452). The very absence of full stops in her soliloquy allows not simply a flow to her thoughts but the recurrence of certain resistances that Molly then maneuvers around. It is as if periods represented something like a weaver's knotting of fabric that is silently unwoven at moments where we would otherwise expect closure.

Of course, the knotting in Joyce is homophonically undone with verbal affirmatives, as Lisa Sternlieb observes: "The first word of her soliloquy—'Yes'—may represent the removal of the first of these knots and every one of the many yeses that follows is another 'not' undone" (Sternlieb 115). In the process, Molly finally escapes the negative implications of masculine definition: "Her overlapping words resist stops, periods, and definitive meanings; she insists on using pronouns so that Bloom, Boylan, and Stephen overlap indistinguishably through the word 'he.' The quotidian and the epic overlap as do the present, past, and future" (Sternlieb 120). In short, her resistance to closely punctuated control allows a flexibility, a capaciousness of consciousness that expands possibility by allowing contradictions and conflicts to emerge.

More than half a century later, a similar embrace of unpunctuated prose occurs in Toni Morrison's *Beloved* (1987), preceded in Chapter 20 with the escaped slave Sethe musing over the ghost of her long-dead child in an anguished monologue: "Beloved, she my daughter. She mine" (Morrison 236). As she recalls having killed Beloved to save her from the unendurable horrors endured by slaves at Sweet Home plantation, we hear her thoughts turn by the end to her second child Denver:

> But the Bodwins got me the cooking job at Sawyer's and left me able to smile on my own like now when I think about you.
>
> But you know all that because you smart like everybody said because when I got here you was crawling already. Trying to get up the stairs. Baby Suggs had them painted white so you could see your way to the top in the dark where lamplight didn't reach. Lord, you loved the stairsteps. (Morrison 240–41)

Immediately following, Sethe's paratactic style is matched in Denver's monologue, beginning with "Beloved is my sister" (Morrison 242), continuing in a stream of consciousness that obsessively goes over the facts of Beloved's return. The whole, expressing how desperately Denver wants to forge a sororal relationship severed by death, ends by recollecting Sethe's motherly advice to her: "She said the ghost was after Ma'am and her too for not doing anything to stop it. But it would never hurt me. I just had to watch out for it because it was a greedy ghost and needed a lot of love" (Morrison 247). Again, phrases emerge in staccato bursts, with emotion trumping calm sequential sense, if finally understandable nonetheless.

By the third monologue, however, punctuation has disappeared nearly altogether as evocation of the dead Beloved's far more fragmented state of mind—understandably so as a ghost of the past:

> I am Beloved and she is mine.   I see her take flowers away from leaves   she puts them in a round basket   the leaves are not for her   she fills the basket   she opens the grass   I would help her but the clouds are in the way   how can I say things that are pictures   I am not separate from her   there is no place where I stop   her face is my own and I want to be there in the place where her face is and to be looking at it too a hot thing. (Morrison 248)

The monologue continues as a patchy account stringing together memory shards, though Morrison assists the reader (in the absence of punctuation marks) by including spacing as here between clauses. That serves to diminish any potential confusion involved in words simply succeeding one another: "again   again   night day   night day   I am waiting   no iron circle is around my neck   no boats go on this water   no men without skin   my dead man is not floating here   his teeth are down there where the blue is and the grass   so is the face I want" (Morrison 251). If the sequence and sense with Beloved prove less obvious or accessible than with her sister's or mother's monologues, uncertainty results less from the absence of punctuation than the confusion of referents, of context and relations.

And the fourth, final monologue, Beloved's once more—"I am Beloved and she is mine" (Morrison 248)—then takes on a more fully embodied form that shifts from punctuated expression into clear sentence form, then into recollected dialogue between Beloved and Sethe arranged by lines, finally to something like poetry integrating the voices of all three women together.

> She said you wouldn't hurt me.
> She hurt me.
> I will protect you.
> I want her face.
> Don't love her too much.
> I am loving her too much.
> Watch out for her; she can give you dreams.
> She chews and swallows.
> Don't fall asleep when she braids your hair.
> She is the laugh; I am the laughter.
> I watch the house; I watch the yard. (Morrison 255)

Here, the unholy trauma of the past seems at least temporarily forestalled via the fragile conventions of punctuation and unsteady end-stopped lines, before the fuller bleak narrative recommences: all as if to confirm that the past has been uncertainly accommodated, shaped for a time by the present into a more adequate accounting.

Unlike Joyce's final Penelope section, where the prose confusion seems driven by Molly's creative ardor, here it seems as if the disruptive effects of Beloved's fragmented emotional state drive the chapter's unpunctuated progress: "as if the text itself were in danger of fragmentation" (Page 134).[1] After all, the entire novel immerses us in the never-ending anguish of the past, the deranged psychology wrought by chattel slavery, leaving no single perspective secure, much less dominant. On the contrary, each of the three main characters (Denver, Sethe, Beloved) wants desperately to possess the other, in an emotional gesture that matches the political tenor of slavery itself. As Jean Wyatt explains:

> The speakers in the three-way dialogue in Beloved reject the separation of persons required by the subject positions of language, where "I" is separate from "you" and "she": they insist on the interpenetration of identities. Consequently, their language erases linguistic demarcations between self and other:

> I have your milk. . . .
> I brought you milk

It is impossible to determine who is speaking: Does the "I" in "I have your milk" refer to Sethe, who might be saying that she "has" (is carrying) Beloved's milk, or to Beloved, who could just as well be the "I" who speaks, saying that she "has" Sethe's milk inside her? The dedifferentiation of possessive pronouns

---

[1] As Page adds:

> The "voices" of the three women, which the reader finally hears on pages 200–217, also cut two ways. On the one hand, their song is a testimony to their intimacy, to their shared sense of family, to their common lives and memories, and their three-in-one union is the most fully developed female triad in Morrison's fiction. But on the other hand, their ingrown dependencies drain away their lives. . . . In fact, their relationships, for all their love, are increasingly possessive. The one word that Stamp can make out is "mine," the key word in each of their monologues. (Page 138–39)

> dramatizes the impossibility of separating what belongs to the
> one body from what belongs to the other when the two are
> joined by the milk that flows between them. (Wyatt 26)

As Wyatt adds about repetition and the problem of identity in
the novel, "Language operates more like interreflecting mirrors
than like dialogue: it exists to assure the speakers that they are
there and they are the same. There is no absence and there is
no difference" (Wyatt 27). Moreover, everything occurs in these
sparsely punctuated monologues in the present tense, matching
the appalling, disorienting nightmare of slavery's Middle Passage
itself—a nightmare whose pain is present long after its enslaving
cause is past. The question left unanswered is how to respond to
this prosaic lack of definition and boundary.

Perfecting a very different defiance of conventional punctuation, the Portuguese Nobel laureate José Saramago embraces
a signature style exemplified in his best-known novel, *Blindness*
(1995). Like most of his fiction, it consists of long, breathless
sentences in which commas take the place of periods, quotation
marks, semicolons, and colons, shaping a heated magma flow of
clauses rushing past. As well, the lack of any quotation marks for
dialogue means that the speakers' identities (or the fact that dialogue is even occurring) is not immediately apparent to the reader, though a change of unnamed speakers is commonly marked
by new capitalization.

Blindness begins with the onset of contagion as a driver all of a
sudden finds himself inexplicably blind, a condition he then mys-
teriously transmits to everyone he meets, leading to a general collapse of government, utilities, civil norms, civilization itself. The
setting is uncertain (though evocative of Portugal), and coupled
with the characters' anonymity contributes a fable-like quality to
the whole, in which the novel offers a rearguard "attempt to avoid
sinking back into a final blindness, a dark blindness, where there
is no love and no stories" (Miller). The question that lingers is
what exactly the epidemic represents, to which the one character saved from blindness, whose fate is to witness the horrors of

all-embracing social collapse, responds: "Why did we become blind, I don't know, perhaps one day we'll find out, Do you want me to tell you what I think, Yes, do, I don't think we did go blind, I think we are blind, Blind but seeing, Blind people who can see, but do not see" (Saramago 326). In short, as Andrew Miller mordantly observes, blindness "is an allegory for not being able to see. What exactly it is we should see, what Saramago—with all his years as a man and a writer and having lived through dictatorship and revolution—fears we cannot see, is present in the writing, present abundantly, but it is not to be paraphrased" (Miller).

That ineffable presence is signaled only gradually in *Blindness*, which opens more or less conventionally, at least in terms of punctuation, with simple and compound sentences intertwined: "The amber light came on. Two of the cars ahead accelerated before the red light appeared. At the pedestrian crossing the sign of a green man lit up" (Saramago 1). But by degrees, as vision is extinguished one by one, the clear sequestering effect of grammatical periods disappears as commas surreptitiously begin to take over:

> The unexpected voice startled the new arrivals, but the two men remained silent, and it was the girl who replied, I think there are four of us, myself and this little boy, Who else, why don't the others speak up, asked the doctor's wife, I'm here, murmured a man's voice, as if he could only pronounce the words with difficulty, And so am I, growled in turn another masculine voice with obvious displeasure. (Saramago 42)

Voices begin to mingle as sentences tumble out unhitched for pages and polyphonic paragraphs extend even longer. The reader's confusion about who is speaking at any given moment more than occasionally matches characters' own blind bewilderment. And though it is Saramago's trademark technique, this run-on style works forcefully (if with little ophthalmic verisimilitude) to evoke what might be envisaged as a figurative condition of sightlessness. Groping in the dark, unable to apprehend verbal milieus, readers are immured as well in an ostensible conversion disorder, of blindness provoked by a "flickering of tense and subject so that we glide between first and third person, between stream of consciousness and wry objectivity" (Miller).

Smoothly shifting between overriding narrative commentary and unsettled individual voices, Saramago scripts a tautly accentuated harmonization of the two. At one moment, we learn of fierce beatings and sheer panic: "they could go neither backwards nor forward, those who were inside, crushed and flattened, tried to protect themselves by kicking and elbowing their neighbours, who were suffocating, cries could be heard, blind children were sobbing, blind mothers were fainting" (Saramago 110). Moments later, the personal anguish is silenced by an eerily calm officialese:

> The arrival of so many blind people appeared to have brought at least one advantage, or, rather, two advantages, the first of these being of a psychological nature, as it were, for there is a vast difference between waiting for new inmates to turn up at any minute, and realising that the building is completely full at last, that from now on it will be possible to establish and maintain stable and lasting relations with one's neighbours, without the disturbances there have been up until now, because of the constant interruptions and interventions by the new arrivals which obliged us to be for ever reconstituting the channels of communication. The second advantage . . . (Saragamo 114)

The contrast between two modes here could not be more dramatic; in the first, of clauses that proliferate full tilt in savage sequence, like blows to the body impossible to ward off; in the second, of phrases that accumulate gradually, slowly diverting attention in the corkscrew periphrasis of rational discourse. As Rhian Atkin observes of this idiosyncratic rhythm, ambiguity is created by switching inconspicuously among registers, sometimes half-a-dozen times a paragraph: "The digressive form of his novels thus serves to emphasize and reiterate their content, highlighting in particular Saramago's constant challenge to grand narratives and official discourses" (Atkin, "Tell" 100). Instead of abstract summations, which feed a regulatory bureaucratic agenda, Saramago invokes a twisting perspective resistant to any adequate generalization itself.

Frequently, the strategy compels rereading, retracing one's steps through "an overflow of language that is never redundant. All of the seeming repetitions are in fact ways of being precise, of continuously searching for yet another way of expressing truth, a truth which although never relative, is certainly always multiple" (de Medeiros 178).[2] The digressions of the novel become increasingly labyrinthine as a means of breaking up not so much a supposedly seamless text but more importantly a putatively neutral, objective perspective. Characters cast doubt on each other's accounts, with exaggeration and embellishment variously exposed, alerting readers actively not to accept blindly all they are told, even by the narrator. Finally, the effect of Saramago's punctuational choices is to confirm that our interpretive efforts must always consist of insight built on a certain constitutional blindness, a condition that seems at first to emerge as a virus but is actually constituent of our identity as readers.

David Frier interprets this bleakly, concluding that "the picture of humanity in *Blindness* is an abject one, with little left towards the end of the text to distinguish the human beings from the scavenging dogs around them in the streets of the city" (Frier, "Righting" 104). Yet one might well demur, guided by the doctor's wife

[2]Though unconcerned with Saramago, Samuel Frederick offers an interpretation of digression useful in reading *Blindness*, arguing against both Seymour Chatman's and Peter Brooks's opposed premises, as either anathema to plot or conversely essential to it: "Instead, I want to show how some radical forms of digression *resist* plot's teleological imperative and its demand for unity, and how, in this resistance, they produce a different mode of storytelling altogether: one in which plot and narrative need not coincide; a narrative freed from the structures of plot" (Frederick 17). Or as he claims: "digression delays not just the end, but also the plot elements that would point *towards* that end. The postponement that results from digressive manoeuvrings, however, is not one that denies satisfaction. Rather, it insists on its own kind of satisfaction *through* this denial" (Frederick 22).

who at the very last seems to waver between the dread of incipient blindness and the flickering prospect of blinding insight: "The city was still there" (Saramago 326). Not only the scene we have before us, but its presentation—in conventionally punctuated clauses that mirror the novel's opening—leave at least a wrinkle in any firm conviction, holding forth the glistening faith that unlike "scavenging dogs" we can indeed learn from having had our sight put in jeopardy. That may prove small consolation, but perhaps adequate to the kind of reading Saramago celebrates: of searching uncertainly for meaning, moving through landscapes of doubt, with any final interpretation left disturbingly unresolved.

Fully as distinguished a writer as Saramago, W. G. Sebald likewise reconfigures punctuation to hammer out a disquieting vision that similarly flouts conventional understanding. His handful of genre-defying works mix memoir, travelogue, and history, magical realism and postmodern pastiche, combining fiction and nonfiction in bearing witness to the Holocaust without reducing it to hackneyed commonplaces or sentimental bromides.[3] Like Saramago, he embraces a diversionary mode, trying to approach a horrifying history without ever risking a direct frontal view:

> I don't think you can focus on the horror of the Holocaust. It's like the head of the Medusa: you carry it with you in a sack, but if you looked at it you'd be petrified. I was trying to write the lives of some people who'd survived—the "lucky ones." If they were so fraught, you can extrapolate. But I didn't see it; I only know things indirectly. (Jaggi)

Again, like Saramago, he distrusts calming notions of presumed objectivity so fully that he resists the very affiliations he so convincingly imagines, or as Maya Jaggi states: "he connects with immense pain, only to say you can't connect; he tries to make you imagine things that he then delicately says are unimaginable" (Jaggi).

---

[3]For deft explanations of Sebald, see Mark Anderson and Maya Jaggi.

Unlike Saramago, however, Sebald persists with one central historical theme in each of four major works, and only gradually, studiously discovers the possibilities of a style that will become fully (or at least, more fully) adequate to it. Arthur Williams has observed, in terms that help explain his punctuational experiments, that "Sebald's oeuvre can be read as a series of threads tied skilfully together, not so much as 'bow ties' . . . but rather as 'stitches' as in knitting or crotchet-work, or, . . . a 'net' or 'mesh,' possibly even a 'snare'" (Williams 27). Of course, the need for such nets occurs because his performances ramble so strenuously, and indirectly, not only in the actual peregrinations of his narratives across foreign shores but in the verbal twists and turns that lead the reader ever afield. His testimony occurs not as finished and systematic account but as ever incomplete fragments, expressing an irresistible vision through what Carol Jacobs calls his "meandering detours, his shattering of frames, crossing borders, writing tangentially, disintegrating the name, surreptitiously citing, and announcing blindness" (Jacobs x). Asked to describe one of Sebald's strangely hybrid books (half fiction, half nonfiction, though the line between is rarely clear), one is hard-pressed to pull the whole together. Or as J. J. Long more critically intones: "The story is not only spun out but is also *clogged up* by the proliferation of inventories and lists, micronarratives and reminiscences, which not only defer the arrival at the end of the main story, but make it impossible to say with any certainty what the main story *is*" (Long 141).

The Rings of Saturn (1995) offers a perfect entry into Sebald's customary habit of surveying history's effects, in describing the walking tour he took through England's Suffolk County, the now-settled site of military resistance to the Nazis that everywhere reminds him of that past. Yet his digressive account ranges from Sir Thomas Browne's skull, to a Rembrandt painting, to sericulture and a gardener amazed at how thoroughly Germans had repressed their own history: "No one at the time seemed to have written about their experiences or afterwards recorded their memories. Even if you asked people directly, it was as if everything had been erased from their minds" (Sebald, *Rings* 39). In the midst of these travels occur musings on Roger Casement and the Belgian Congo, a link to thoughts of Swinburne, a review of the Irish Troubles in 1920, even a wooden model of the Temple of Jerusalem.

But invariably, reflections, allusions, and alleged facts of the Third Reich intrude, intersecting with images that thread through each of the ten chapters, prompting a shock of recognition about an actual burgeoning silk industry in Germany that curiously paralleled the buildup of Nazi concentration camps. Throughout, Sebald strangely avoids paragraphing, even though he still divides the whole into ten unequivocal chapters.[4] As well, frequently drawing on photographs, he converts them into a singular form of punctuation, of odd landscapes with armaments placed mid-sentence to mildly alter the text, enhancing "the melancholic tone . . . , the feeling the reader has that it is always grey and rainy" (Jarosz 24). More importantly, Sebald relies (as Saramago never does) on the pause evoked by dashes, pauses that erupt infrequently but that nonetheless punctuate an emotional silence. Late in *Rings*, he suffers through a sandstorm that evokes for him the great British storm of 1987 not simply as an immense natural disaster (fourteen million trees upended) but as reminder of human impotence in the face of meteorological as well as historical and geopolitical forces:

> Gasping for breath, my mouth and throat dry, I crawled out of the hollow that had formed around me like the last survivor of a caravan that had come to grief in the desert. A deathly silence prevailed. There was not a breath, not a birdsong to be

---

[4]There are, as it happens, two paragraphs on p. 59, one on p. 64—both of which seem as arbitrary as their absence earlier. See also the paragraphs on pp. 80, 85, 88, 89, 90, 92, 96; 104, 105, and then only occasionally and ever more sparsely on pp. 259, 278, 286, 289, 294. As Ceri Radford has observed, "Jane Austen didn't write in paragraphs, which were inserted by editors. Nor did Jack Kerouac tapping out *On the Road* in three weeks on a 120-foot-long scroll of paper. In both cases, only the manuscripts point to a certain breathlessness" (Radford).

> heard, not a rustle, nothing. And although it now grew lighter
> once more, the sun, which was at its zenith, remained hidden
> behind the banners of a pollen-fine dust that hung for a long
> time in the air. This, I thought, will be what is left after the
> earth has ground itself down. —I walked the rest of the way in
> a daze. (Sebald, *Rings* 229)

The extended series of brief clauses builds to and trails off from
the "deathly silence" in a scene that at once stands free of any
past and yet whose imagery once more evokes the horror of Nazi
ideology. Even so, the scene is split off by a dash from Sebald's
resumption of his walking tour. As Nathan Goldman writes: "The
dash invites the reader to pause—to linger for a moment. The
earth bereft of life—can we imagine such a thing? The dash creates a space to encounter, or at least to attempt to encounter, the
notion's terrible sublimity" (Goldman).

Perhaps the most dramatic use of the dash occurs in the closing discussion of silkworm production as a perfect cultural model
for "the best and cleanest of all possible worlds," at least as it was
understood in prewar Germany (Sebald, *Rings* 292). If "silk-
worms afforded an almost ideal object lesson for the classroom,"
they also were "taken by breeders to monitor productivity and
selection, including extermination to preempt racial degeneration.—In the film, we see a silk-worker receiving eggs despatched
by the Central Reich Institute of Sericulture in Celle, and depos-
iting them in sterile trays . . . and so on until the entire killing
business is completed" (Sebald, *Rings* 294). Sebald uses this kind
of dash repeatedly to "signify breaks in the narrative," but breaks
so severe, as Nathan Goldman points out:

> as an attempt to capture the horror of what the words that pre-
> cede and follow it only allude to. The dash, situated between
> the talk of schoolroom sericulture and the talk of silkworm
> execution, creates a moment of silence—the very opposite of
> talk—for the victims of the death camps. It's Sebald's attempt
> to make legible a loss that language can circle but never quite
> reach. (Goldman)

These occasional dashes in *Rings of Saturn* erupt into the text, suggesting all the ways in which dislocations occur between present memory and past trauma, immediate recollection and initiating pain. And in so doing, they afford a brief respite for the reader to contemplate the troubling junctures of interlinked, often bizarre ruminations.

Sebald resists any simple accommodation to the past even as he draws on the very means by which accommodation might be reached: photograph, montage, intertextual allusion, even a mix of nostalgic reminiscence and Orwellian bureaucratese. For while the past is silent, having left only traces behind, the need to pause before those traces in order to grant them room to speak, rather than being simply ventriloquized by a self-satisfied present, remains Sebald's steadfast conviction. The past, after all, has created him (as a German born in the war to a soldier for the Third Reich). Not until the transition to *Austerlitz* (2001), however, did he feel equal to offering an account of what he judged to be the wasteland of his life, "of the destructive effect on me of my desolation through all those past years" (Sebald, *Austerlitz* 137). The whole encompasses his anxiety attacks, severe mental distress, and suppressed memories in a continuous prose sequence, with one single paragraph (p. 88), and in a sequence that has abandoned divisions by chapters, though relying on asterisks three times instead for sectional divisions (pp. 32, 117, 254; with a white space on p. 290). Overall, as well, his sentences linger on ceaselessly much longer than in earlier work.

Still, his obsession remains similar. Instead of a walking tour through Suffolk that evokes the effects of the Holocaust, however, he stands aside from his own autobiographical musings, becoming instead the imagined narrator of a displaced self, his equally peripatetic friend, Jacques Austerlitz (though we are never quite sure whether this figure was actually real or not). Raised by foster parents in Wales, Austerlitz belatedly learns he was secreted as an infant refugee away from the Nazis by his biological parents, later killed in the camps. In the course of recounting his research of their fates, Austerlitz reveals his own continuing sense of

abandonment, his subsequent nervous breakdown, the discovery
of an elderly nanny now in Prague, and the propaganda video he
obtains of the Theresienstadt concentration camp where he thinks
he recognizes a clip of his mother. Like Sebald, he continues to feel
a failure, worried that his sketches were "misguided, distorted,
and of little use," leaving him "increasingly overcome by a sense
of aversion and distaste, said Austerlitz" (Sebald, *Austerlitz* 121).
Or as he, an architectural historian, ponders the analogy between
language and urban sprawl:

> If language may be regarded as an old city full of streets
> and squares, nooks and crannies, with some quarters dat-
> ing from far back in time while others have been torn down,
> cleaned up, and rebuilt, and with suburbs reaching further
> and further into the surrounding country, then I was like a
> man who has been abroad a long time and cannot find his
> way through this urban sprawl anymore, no longer knows
> what a bus stop is for, or what a back yard is, or a street junc-
> tion, an avenue or a bridge. The entire structure of language,
> the syntactical arrangement of parts of speech, punctuation,
> conjunctions, and finally even the nouns denoting ordinary
> objects were all enveloped in impenetrable fog. (Sebald, *Aus-
> terlitz* 123–24)

Moreover, the architectonics of Sebald's sentences themselves
reflect this breakdown: with clauses that fold back or digress;
with multiple levels of narration signaled by the use of inquit
("said Austerlitz"), often mid-sentence, or even double inquit
("said Vera, Austerlitz added"); and again, with photographs that
sometimes validate, at others deviate from the sentences they
interrupt.

It is as if the Nazi horror emerges only glancingly through isolate moments in the text, seen briefly before Austerlitz returns
to another digression, admits to additional failure, surveys the
imperiously out-sized architecture of modernist Europe that
forms the continuing heritage of the Third Reich. As Mark

McCulloh has observed, "the detachment of the narrative approach, not unlike that of Kafka's, seems to be an integral part of Sebald's authorial strategy, since he is obviously determined to look at everything anew, with the eyes of an extraterrestrial who is experiencing the susceptibilities of life on earth for the first time" (McCulloh 82). Or as McCulloh adds, "the fascination elicited by his kaleidoscopic continuum of associations" is enhanced by the erasure of history and memory that lies at the heart of Sebald's vision (McCulloh 82). The diversionary, digressive syntax that keeps swiveling us among disconnected moments and fractious observations stands as implicit critique of the relentless, inflexible monumentalism of Nazi ideology. Style, from this perspective, condemns the world it evokes inadvertently.

That is, it does so with one telling exception: near the close, having discovered a Nazi account by H. G. Adler of Theresienstadt, Austerlitz reproduces a photographed list tersely describing camp jobs. In an eight-page sentence, he then mimics the horrifying, emotionless Nazi view in a desiccated recitation of the grueling conditions under which prisoners were forced to work. The orderly, calculated meticulousness of the sentence induces deepening unease, as we learn "of the precinct mending and darning rooms, the shredding section, the rag depot, the book reception and sorting unit, the kitchen brigade, the potato-peeling platoon, the bone-crushing mill, the glue-boiling plant, or the mattress department, as medical and nursing auxiliaries, in the disinfestation and rodent control service, the floor space allocation office" and so on (Sebald, *Austerlitz* 237). The apparently detached mode is the sole reaction possible to the barbaric "final solution" implemented by the Nazis, then carried out with "crazed administrative zeal" (Sebald, *Austerlitz* 241). But we also realize that this description is made from Austerlitz's perspective, suggesting his own run-on helplessness in the face of what he depicts. Sebald's prose narrative ends precipitously, with no summary conclusion, before Austerlitz has presumably learned the mystery of his father's death. All we are left with is a sense of deplorably silent indeterminacy in the face of history's horrors. Though as Tholeif Persson concludes about all of Sebald's melancholy efforts, "the central issue at stake is the relationship between the ethics of representation and the politics of remembrance" (Persson 205).[5]

[5]The postmodern novelist who most resembles Sebald in his bleak vision and punctuational experimentation is the Hungarian László Krasznahorkai. Throughout, he extends his sentences interminally, dissolving the boundaries of narrative voices, until in *The Last Wolf* (2009), he unfolds the entire seventy-six-page novella in a single epic sentence, unbroken by paragraphs. His sentences, admired the 2015 Man Booker judges, "like a lint roll, pick up all sorts of odd and unexpected things as they accumulate inexorably into paragraphs that are as monumental as they are scabrous and musical" (Nowell). He is among the better recent writers who, in James Wood's words, concentrate:

> on filling the sentence, using it to notate and reproduce the tiniest qualifications, hesitations, intermittences, affirmations and negations of being alive. This is one reason that very long, breathing, unstopped sentences, at once literary and vocal, have been almost inseparable from the progress of experimental fiction since the nineteen-fifties. Claude Simon, Thomas Bernhard, José Saramago, W. G. Sebald, Roberto Bolaño, David Foster Wallace, James Kelman, and László Krasznahorkai have used the long sentence to do many different things, but all of them have been at odds with a merely grammatical realism, whereby the real is made to fall into approved units and packets. (Wood, "Madness")

7

Enjambment: Cummings, Williams, Giovanni

Surprising as it sounds, prose may well be more readily left un-punctuated than poetry, though poets have a longer modern history of experimenting with an absence of marks. And when they do, it is often because line breaks serve as a form of disguised punctuational guide or, in Charles O. Hartman's words, "as a kind of master punctuation mark" (Hartman 153). Arguably as well, the less punctuation poetry exhibits, the less simply verbal it seems to become and the more its impact verges on the visual, which may explain the allure of shaped or pattern poems (sometimes known as visual or concrete poetry) that burst into prominence in the mid-twentieth century. Typographical marks convey meaning in poems as much ocular as rhetorical, whose effect is thereby largely lost when read aloud. Yet short of such experiments, poets often enjamb lines or drop capitalization and periods, evincing poetic statements with neither pauses nor caesuras.[1]

---

[1]Phil Provance has observed:

> Usually a lack of punctuation creates what might be described as "internal enjambment," or in other words, it "annotates" the line by making two phrases seem to flow into each other, providing multiple ways to read the line. Another use, as seen in Frank O'Hara's "Lana Turner Has Collapsed" is to speed up a line, as if the speaker is whipping through the language quickly; the effect in O'Hara's poem is to create a snarky, sarcastic rhythm, in other words, a "short" delivery in the sense of "being short"/"being snide." Finally, if punctuation would fall in the line break but isn't there the purpose of omitting it is frequently to prevent the reader from pausing

A trio of American poets has been drawn to this structural possibility out of a shared resistance to conventional modes, though for reasons that curiously happen to be diametrically opposed. E. E. Cummings, William Carlos Williams, and Nikki Giovanni each embraced the freedom of abandoning punctuation, with its assorted implications, and in the process offer a sharp contrast not only to other figures in this study but distinctively to each other. Cummings turned from conventional punctuation as a means of exploring what otherwise seemed hidden, the visual realms of poetry; Williams did so out of a radical reconception of the relation between image and referent; Giovanni did so out of a desire to perfect an exhortatory, distinctively oral mode. Yet each of these three anticipated the wonderfully fruitful ambiguities generated by a lack of punctuation in poems, especially with regard to agency and perspective. Indeed, Cummings resisted marks so assiduously that he published under the sobriquet e e cummings, while Giovanni reframed stanzaic conventions in an effort to proclaim a distinctive black consciousness. Along with Williams, their poems establish borders where punctuation might forcefully seem to detract from rather than add to a poetic resonance. And from this perspective, it is as if Cummings and Williams, who each admired the other immensely, helped prepare the way for Giovanni's success in an entirely different formal venture.

Cummings is usually associated with the modernist turn toward free-form poetry, following rhythms of natural speech to delight in whimsical possibilities of verbal and visual play. Indeed, the visual at times seemed to overtake the verbal, as Marianne Moore exuberantly proclaimed: "The physique of the poems recalls the corkscrew twists, the infinitude of dots, the sumptuous

---

longer than the break itself before heading to the next line, an option that may be used for rhythmic purposes (since a line break is already a "quarter break" in a music analogy, a comma at a break is equivalent to a period or semi-colon, roughly), but also, if a subsequent line has a "back-enjambed" line through caesura (i.e., when a word or phrase is set off alone at the start of a line, forcing the reader to read it both as part of the preceding syntax AND as itself alone) the effect is often to create speed to that line whose phrasing may create a double-entendre, in addition to being emphatic. (Provance)

perpendicular appearance of Kufic script . . ." (Moore 47).[2] Over time, he would even abandon the conventional syntax and capitalization of his early stanzaic poems, often in celebrating a spirit of carpe diem.

In his celebrated poem "since feeling is first," from his second collection, *Is5* (1926), Cummings expresses a belief in the primacy of emotion over reason, part of a perfectly recognizable romantic tenet:

> since feeling is first
> who pays any attention
> to the syntax of things
> will never wholly kiss you;
> wholly to be a fool
> while Spring is in the world
>
> my blood approves
> and kisses are a better fate
> than wisdom
> lady i swear by all flowers. Don't cry
> —the best gesture of my brain is less than
> your eyelids' flutter which says
>
> we are for each other: then
> laugh, leaning back in my arms
> for life's not a paragraph
>
> and death i think is no parenthesis (*CP* 291)

[2]As she had already proclaimed rhapsodically:

> One has in Mr. Cummings' work, a sense of the best dancing and the best horticulture. . . . Settling like a man-of-war bird or the retarded, somnambulistic athlete of the speedograph, he shapes the progress of poems as if it were substance; he has "a trick of syncopation Europe has," determining the pauses slowly, with glides and tight-rope acrobatics, ensuring the ictus by a space instead of a period, or a semicolon in the middle of a word, seeming to have placed adjectives systematically one word in advance of the words they modify, or one word behind, with most pleasing exactness. (Moore 46)

Love's essential nature, so Cummings would have it, emerges less as a matter of acquired knowledge than irrepressible passion ("kisses are a better fate / than wisdom"), corresponding at first glance to the poem's uniform lack of studied capitalization, along with its minimal punctuation: a semicolon, period, dash, and a colon, which finally seem themselves unneeded.[3] The series of individual marks affords a fourfold template for what might be assessed as outmoded punctuational guides, each used only once as if vestigially. And while the whole is set up with "since," as part of a potential argument requiring "then," the second line immediately dismisses any need for so conventional a sequential logic.

Yet both the presence and the lack of punctuation unsettles our initial assumptions, immediately seeming to require a rereading. The first hesitation occurs with the doubling of "wholly" on either side of a semicolon, which at first might suggest the continuation of a thought but in this case seems to disrupt it. The initial "wholly" relies on a partner who seems bound by "the syntax of things"; the second starts by linking to that partner, then all but immediately pivots to the poet himself, ready to insert himself in this dynamic, eager "to be a fool." Then his desire for rational argument suddenly reasserts itself, in an effort to convince his love that "kisses are a better fate." That forms the apparent link between the first and the second stanzas, as if the capitalized "Spring" of the first jump-started the emotional gesture of the second.

[3]As Rushworth Kidder has noted of the "rules" for reading Cummings, a reader should "*Supply punctuation and capitalization as necessary.* Cummings often deletes periods, commas, colons, and quotation marks, which need to be reinserted by the reader" (Kidder 11). Alternatively, in many of Cummings's later poems, he brandishes punctuation in unusual ways, sometimes within words themselves. Norman Friedman argues that Cummings is

upgathering, leaping, disintegrating, and rearranging. . . . partially by the distribution of parentheses, punctuation marks, and capitals; and partially by the joining, splitting, and spacing of words. The over-all intent, then, is not primarily visual at all, but rather figurative and aesthetic . . . to loosen up the effect of a metrical line, to suggest the thing or idea spoken of, to alter and reinforce meanings, or to amplify and retard. (Friedman 124; see also 114–16)

Even in so simple a poem, the wonder lies in how fully it becomes self-referential. Incorporating the very punctuation it denies as a theme at the end, with two neat five-line stanzas reduced
to a three-line suspension, then a one-line conclusion, it shows
form itself breaking down in confirmation of the poem's delicate
(mildly erotic, amusingly linguistic) resonances.[4] The question
raised by the second line of "who pays any attention" becomes
the calling card of the poem, though each line then incrementally
alters what has come before. And by the end, we realize that "life's
not a paragraph," in any sense able to be constrained by rule, nor
is it contained by the customary "parenthesis" of death. The in-
determinacies of punctuation, or its lack, seem to press along
in the rush of erotic emotion that carries an argument against
grammatical rule.[5] As Rushworth Kidder remarks of the obvious
reading of "abandon" celebrated by the poem: "Feeling, for Cummings, may well be 'first' over logic; but the poet in this poem
bends this idea to his own ends with a logical skill carefully calculated to ensnare his prey" (77). In fact, the central stanza encapsulates the speaker's emotional declaration as a moment of defiance,
dismissing "syntax" in the very addition of punctuation (period,
capitalization, dash) with end-stopped lines making themselves

[4]William Heyen wants

> to read this poem as though it speaks better than its speaker knows. I want
> to say that its essential thrust is its duplicity. I want to say that Cummings
> does not go as far as many of his critics have said he has gone in denying
> rationality, intelligence, logic; that these abstractions are indeed his
> whipping boys, but in a more complex way than Cummings has been
> given credit for. (Heyen 233)

As he adds, "the poem can be read as a defense of spontaneous poetry, as a
confrontation between poet and muse. What it should not be read as is a blanket
condemnation of rationality" (Heyen 234).

[5]Richard Kennedy observes: "Cummings liked to startle whenever he could. The
parentheses around 'Do you think?' [in his first poem ever] do not belong there;
they belong in the next line, surrounding the intruded phrase 'i do'" (Kennedy
2). And Kennedy later adds: "At times Cummings violates typographical norms
only to be different—as with the comma that begins line ten, or the oddly placed
period in line thirteen" (Kennedy 8).

as clear syntactically as enjambed ones. Strangely, we realize that syntax *does* matter in the ways the stanza seems akilter, matching the ebullient fashion in which the speaker wants to win his lady.

Cummings, lighthearted and relatively easygoing in this jeu d'esprit, is clearly not changing our fundamental vision of love, nor the meaning of words, nor the shifting poetics of conventional usage. Typographic marks may be removed like summer clothes, but that doesn't quite alter our understanding of the way words work in his poems. "Tumbling-hair" (1923), however (from his first collection, *Tulips & Chimneys*), presents a potentially darker, mythically more resonant scenario in the image of a child simply picking flowers:

> Tumbling-hair
>> picker of buttercups
>>> violets
> dandelions
> And the big bullying daisies
>> through the field wonderful
> with eyes a little sorry
> Another comes
>> also picking flowers (*CP* 31)

Unlike the earlier poem, here the lineation alters, with spatial pauses adjusting our sense of lines as we read, even as each line seems end-stopped with punctuation simply removed (mostly commas), or a verb (before "through the field wonderful" with the long indentation allowing a reader's open choice among possible verbs).[6] We shift from "tumbling-hair / picker," assumed to be a child roaming through a field, to a scene in which small flowers are succeeded by "big bullying daisies" that somehow lead us

---

[6]Daniel Matore has pointed out that "'The negative doubt implicit in typographical blanks, their frailty of dimension, is what their prosodic value is predicated upon. Prosody is a current that is not reducible to any single type of sonic or visual content—intonation, pitch, accent, or quantity become prosodic by assuming meaningful contours, but prosody itself transcends these given incarnations of it" (Matore 1528).

into "eyes a little sorry." Moreover, the poem's abbreviation along with its lack of punctuation makes it hard to understand where aggression begins and ends—whether *with* the daisies or beyond ("through the field wonderful"). Only the final determinate turn to "Another comes" suggests the arrival of an eery additional presence, possibly death or the tumbler herself grown older or even the poet himself. In every case, however, the way "through the field wonderful" of childhood delight is necessarily evanescent, while the descriptive "through" reveals itself as ambivalent syntactically, tilting between "big bullying daisies" and "eyes a little sorry."

The poem's very brevity; its lack of any punctuation other than three capitalizations that seem to register new sentences, though without accompanying periods; its curious depersonalization amid a floral landscape—all contribute to a certain allegorical resonance in which agency disappears, with a curious admixture of sexuality and death linked somehow to childhood innocence. Looming behind the scene is the Greek myth of Persephone, the young goddess of spring abducted by Hades as she was picking flowers, then taken against her will to the Underworld. But the poem also invokes the idea of death as God's gardener, a tender of souls, who cuts life short at moments when we are taken aback, heedless and unaware. And even the flowering sequence registers a rise in narrative tension nowhere else apparent, from buttercups to timid (delayed) violets, then dandelions pushing to the head of the line, displaced by "bullying daisies" (a bloom like violets usually associated with innocence and purity). The absence of punctuation, moreover, leads to the ambivalence of "eyes a little sorry"—as perhaps the figurative yellow eyes of the daisies immediately preceding the phrase, or of the "Another" who also comes to gather flowers.[7] More than most of Cummings's poems, this

---

[7]Richard Kennedy states:

> The lack of punctuation in the poem allows for a double reading of one of the phrases: the daisies are "through the field wonderful," but "wonderful" can also modify another noun: "through the field wonderful ... / Another comes." The capital "A" on "Another" begins to give mythic significance

one holds back from clear paraphrase, teetering on the edge of a tradition that returns ineluctably to the classic scene, extending from Homer through Milton and Tennyson to Louise Glück. As even enthusiasts acknowledge of Cummings: "The style almost always employs novel images, simple diction, casual conversational phrasing and syntax, and a visual form that moves slowly along to create its delicate impression or modest assertion" (Kennedy 5).

The enigmatic absence of punctuation in Cummings prompts one to wonder at the alternative, when poetic markings are by contrast deliberately included, even indulged in overabundance. As it happens, Cummings himself wondered at the possibility, most famously in "r-p-o-p-h-e-s-s-a-g-r" (1935). The poem went through multiple drafts in which he altered its radically conceived punctuation, exchanging one mark for another, revising spacings, indentations, capitalizations, and combinations. From its title on, in fact, it hardly seems like any poem we have seen before.

```
                    r-p-o-p-h-e-s-s-a-g-r
              who
     a)s w(e loo)k
     upnowgath
              PPEGORHRASS
                                  eringint(o-
     aThe):l
           eA
             !p:
     S                                        a
                    (r
     rIvInG                    .gRrEaPsPhOs)
                                        to
     rea(be)rran(com)gi(e)ngly
     ,grasshopper;
```

to the scene in the same way that myth entered the poem about the "balloonMan." The final phrase, "also picking flowers," refers us back to the beginning, and we realize as the poem comes to a close, that she is the flower that he will pick. (Kennedy 22)

A first reading defies comprehension, though clearly punctuation itself dominates any possible meaning, with hyphens, parentheses, capitalization, colons, semicolons, even spacing dictating what can hardly be read, much less expressed orally as a poem.

By the last line, we encounter a named grasshopper (the only distinct word other than "who" in the poem) and realize in turn that it has been named anagrammatically three earlier times (including the title). As Sam Hynes first noted, the poem is not so much about a grasshopper but

> about an object which becomes a grasshopper in the course of the poem. In the first line it is simply something, in the grass or on a twig, extended (lower case letters separated by dashes) but unidentified. But as we glance toward it (the double take, in two quick parentheses) it draws itself together, becomes taller and more condensed—becomes a definite and particular object, a The. It leaps, and we follow its course with our eyes, from S to a. A grasshopper's leap is a sudden, startling thing, and so there is an exclamation point imbedded in the word.

> The thing, the The, lands, in an attitude halfway between the contraction just preceding the leap and the extension of the first line. Now we see him clearly, and as we look he rearranges himself to become a grasshopper. (Hynes)

The poem, in short, resists being read rather than seen as a mental sequence, "a picture of an action rather than a description of it" (Hynes), imaging each part of the grasshopper's leap as if realized simultaneously. That helps explain the exclamation point and colon in the middle of "leA!p:S" and the superimposition of the penultimate line of "become" over "rearrangingly": "rea(be) rran(com)gi(e)ngly." It also explains the precise configuration of each anagrammatical variation, with the first ("r-p-o-p-h-e-s-s-a-g-r") instance suggesting a certain alienating abstraction, an unrecognizable, physically articulated (thus hyphenated) object. The second reference occurs all in uppercase ("PPEGORHRASS"), bringing to mind, according to Vakrilen Kilyovski, "the maximum muscle tension of the 'beast' at the precise millisecond of its leaping off the ground" (Kilyovski 103). What begins as a jumble of punctuation between and amid an assortment of apparently random letters becomes a visual poem, radically reorienting our sense of poetry itself. As Cummings admitted: "not all of my poems are to be read aloud—some . . . are to be seen & not heard" (*Letters* 267).[8] Yet as Brian Gingrich admits, even in this extreme case we "keep bouncing back (and forth) from the visual-pictorial appearance of the poem to an attempt to ‘read’ it nevertheless— as if reading now means something more like deciphering, seeing the letters not as images/icons but as symbols, and deciphering now includes not just the letters but the punctuation marks too" (Gingrich private correspondence).

William Carlos Williams strongly admired Cummings, esteeming him along with Ezra Pound as "the two most distinguished American poets" of his time (MacLeod 31). As it happens, however, Williams's own efforts with an unpunctuated visual style tend to be even more radical than Cummings's. Stripping out what he regarded as extraneous syntactical marks, he strove to forgo a long tradition of poetry that presumed a descriptive relationship with the natural world. Williams himself declared that "Design makes things speak. In *Spring and All*, these two concepts are in creative friction. The book rejects 'verisimilitude, that great copying' as plagiarism of nature, insisting instead on a 'separation. The word must be put down for itself, not as a symbol of nature but as a part, cognizant of the whole'" (Costello). Williams achieved this appositional vision of art, no longer contingent on a predetermining natural world, largely through meter and line. And by experimenting in particular with enjambment even more severe than Cummings's, he focused attention on the isolate shimmering of individual words themselves, words like "wheelbarrow" and "plums."

---

[8]For excellent analyses of this poem, see as well Gillian Huang-Tiller and Michael Walker.

Throughout a long career, Williams would regularly include punctuation, though it is worth attending to what happens when he resists its structuring appeal, as in one of his better-known early poems, "The Great Figure" (1921) (*SP* 36):

Among the rain
and lights
I saw the figure 5
in gold
on a red
firetruck
moving
tense
unheeded
to gong clangs
siren howls
and wheels rumbling
through the dark city.

Here, the poem emerges as a long, complex sentence, beginning with capitalization and ending with a period in traditional format. But the hourglass shape of the whole consists of five lines of opening clauses and four of closing ones, separated by four lines that slow our reading to concentrate on single words detached from the other. The effect is to focus attention on words *as* words, not referring to something other than their own linguistic resonance but as "black letters on a white page," in Peter Halter's description; "words that can be moved around on the page so as to form a pattern and become part of a design" (Halter 47).[9]

---

[9] J. Hillis Miller earlier had commented:

> The simplicity of the sentence structure here, and the emphasis on the tensions between the words makes them stand separate and yet together. Rhythm also works to achieve this end. Williams's metrical effects have an extraordinary power to bring each word out in its "thingness," to make the reader pause over it and savor its tang before going on to the next word. . . . The independence of the words in the poem matches the independence

The very isolation of a word in a line lends it a certain lustrous power, defying the grammatical connections that might leach away its sound and bite into the words hemming it in. As well, the lack of punctuation that enforces the poem's enjambment contributes to an ongoing slippage of verbal meaning even as words join each other: "clangs/siren"; "howls/and wheels"; "rumbling/ through the dark city."[10] The painting that Williams's good friend Charles Demuth made of the poem, *I Saw the Figure 5 in Gold* (1928), captures the poetic resonances with pictorial flair, tripling (or more) the number 5, breaking the fire engine into red blocks, incorporating Williams's names ("Bill," "Carlo") as part of the poetic valance. And the angled forms of this "poster portrait" nicely match the poem's own angling.

Williams had already returned the favor in "The Pot of Flowers" (1922) (*SP* 40), conceived of as a "painted poem" inspired by Demuth's *Tuberoses* (1922) in a self-conscious effort, as he conceded, "to fuse the poetry and painting, to make it the same thing" (Costello). Yet the poem is not a literal transcription or otherwise ekphrastic, since various details decidedly differ. In a far more radical gesture, Williams matches Demuth's visual performance of removing the flowers from a garden setting; "he floats and isolates them in empty space," James Breslin observes, "at once permitting him to define their contours with sharp, distinct lines, yet to remind us that these objects *are* abstracted, lifted from *any* context, for heightened aesthetic contemplation; the space they dwell in is an *artistic* space" (Breslin 251). Williams's parallel effort suspends words rather than colors and shapes, though to the similar end of defining an autonomous world of art. As Breslin

of the things they name. The short lines and brief monosyllables of Williams's verse have exactly the opposite effect from the long rapidly rolling blurred periods of Whitman's line, with its tendency to absorb all particulars into one sonorous whole. (Miller 39)

[10]As Charles O. Hartman has observed of another poem: "By dissolving a little of the syntactic glue that holds the poem's sentence together line breaks paradoxically enable connections across wider stretches of language" (Hartman 154).

remarks of Williams's habitual declaration that poems are made of words and the spaces between them:

> Notice how he says "words and the *spaces*"—not "pauses," as we might expect a poet to do—but *spaces,* as if a poem were first of all a physical, a visual, object . . . More important, "words and the spaces between them" suggests an esthetic clearly enacted in the short, broken lines of the poems, an esthetic that is concerned with isolating objects in space—in order (as in Demuth) to keep them distinct. (Breslin 252)

Context seems defied in the poem, with colors, shades, light itself "contending" with the "dark" pot.

It is as if words do not so much recover a spatialized moment or remind us of an elaborate floral scene as register a disconnected series of referents, independently incandescent, pointing to nothing but themselves as autonomous verbal forms in space focused by the poet's intense gaze and stunningly sensitized ear:

> Pink confused with white
> flowers and flowers reversed
> take and spill the shaded flame
> darting it back
> into the lamp's horn
>
> petals aslant darkened with mauve
>
> red where in whorls
> petal lays its glow upon petal
> round flamegreen throats
> petals radiant with transpiercing light
> contending
>   above
> the leaves
> reaching up their modest green
> from the pot's rim
>
> and there, wholly dark, the pot
> gay with rough moss.

Instead of single or one-word lines (with a solitary exception), stanzas of varying lengths, varying words, varying spaces tumble down the page. The inversion of "flowers and flowers reversed" enhances the word as word, almost encouraging the reader to imagine it reversed into "srewolf" (occurring again with "petal lays its glow upon petal"). The eye-rhyme of "darting" and "darkened" increases the verbal resonance, as does "where in whorls." Moreover, the spatial pause at "above" splits the poem all but in two, if likewise binding the two parts together with that verbal splice. The curious effect of Williams's placement of prepositions, as here, or adjectives and conjunctions alone or at the end of a line is to focus our eye on these otherwise, seemingly subsidiary, suturing lexemes as themselves substantive, just as forceful in their meaning as any verb or noun.

Williams's agenda may be even better appreciated in two versions of a later poem, "The Locust Tree in Flower" (*SP* 93). The first, written in 1933, is lesser known, with only one dash as punctuation coming precisely midway through the eight stanzas, each three lines long. And the question remains why the dash (along with capitalization) remains:

Among
the leaves
bright

green
of wrist-thick
tree

and old
stiff broken
branch

ferncool
swaying
loosely strung—

come May

again
white blossom

clusters
hide
to spill

their sweets
almost
unnoticed

down
and quickly
fall

The poem is carefully balanced and enjambed throughout, moving in a sprightly rhythm (half iambic, half trochaic) as if in celebration of the newly pointed (hence "bright green") leaves and the drooping clusters of fragile white flowers. The dash splicing the whole together by halves serves to join the mid-May construction of this tree. Of course, the poem even so offers a more or less conventional presentation of vernal attributes, yet set off with short lines and jaunty diction, including the compound neologisms "ferncool" and "wrist-thick." Again, like Cummings he delights in single-word lines, but mixes up single and double as if to let us off the leash then pull us gently back to a tighter concentration.

The second version (*SP* 94), written two years later, reduces the whole from eight stanzas to ten stark lines of only thirteen words. Dropping earlier figurative language along with all but one possible verb ("come"), the new version prompts us to wonder after reading the first what is gained by this fine-tuned verbal dismantling.

Among
of
green

stiff
old
bright

broken
branch
come
white
sweet
May

again

Most obviously, Williams succeeds in his ongoing effort to make our viewing of words restricted to their performance *as* individual words, breaking linkages between parts of speech. The opening simply disarms the reader in the standoff between prepositions, as if it were undecided about how to launch itself, caught between two alternatives: being in the midst of, yet separate from, other parts versus being identified with those very parts themselves. Do we begin as abiding in the green environ or somehow apart from it? Without answering, the poem moves us word by word through "the locust tree in flower," as if in a random set of observational accretions shorn of syntactic placement, requiring a reader's sprightly assist. The line breaks and apparently missing punctuation compel us simply to contemplate the sequence of "broken / branch / come," pausing to pull the images into alignment with diction, registering this flowering as an experience once "again."

Few have come closer than J. Hillis Miller to the delight of the poem, as it establishes what is most distinctive about so full a concentration on single words shorn of punctuation:

The words hang freely in the air. Moreover, the verb presupposes a plural subject, so the reader must balance between the possibility that the word "has" may have been left out and the assumption that "come" is to be taken as an imperative. This grammatical uncertainty forces him to hold all the words before his attention at once as he tries various ways to make a sentence of them. He is like a seal juggling thirteen brightly colored balls, and this is exactly what the poet wants. The poem is as much all there at once as the locust tree itself, in its tension of branches, leaves, and flowers. The poem is not a picture of the tree, but is itself something substantial echoing in its structure of verbal forces the birth of white blossoms from stiff boughs. (Miller 45)

In short, words do not stand for anything outside themselves, or otherwise (at least at their most irresistible) mean anything but themselves. We turn to them, especially in the more cherished realms of poetry, for their sound, their shape, their distinctive place in our vocabulary that so rarely seems so distinctive. And one way to foreground that importance was to get rid of punctuation altogether, any marks that slowed words down, or stopped them, or reversed their course. That condition lay at the heart of a robustly concentrated poetic vision.

Williams had an immense influence on subsequent poets of every stripe, though few abandoned punctuation entirely in their various efforts. Perhaps the most important of his legatees, Nikki Giovanni transformed that legacy in largely confessional poems that first grew out of the Black Arts Movement of the 1960s, which shared a resolutely militant African-American perspective. Unlike Cummings, focused on tight, visually configured poems, or Williams, in his devotion to the import of individual words, Giovanni has concentrated throughout her career on poetry's distinctively oral qualities and its performative possibilities.[11] As effectively as any of her poems, "Habits" (1978) (*CP* 262–63) lays out what would become her main concerns:

---

[11]For the best assessment of Giovanni's developing interest in poetry as oral performance, see Virginia Fowler (*Literary Biography* 57 ff.).

i haven't written a poem in so long
i may have forgotten how
unless writing a poem
is like riding a bike
or swimming upstream
or loving you
it may be a habit that once acquired
is never lost

but you say I'm foolish
of course you love me
but being loved of course
is not the same as being loved because
or being loved despite
or being loved

if you love me why
do i feel so lonely
and why do i always wake up alone
and why am i practicing
not having you to love
i never loved you that way

The absence of punctuation, a half-century after the lead of Cummings and Williams, veers admittedly nowhere close to the disorienting landscapes of their poems. Perhaps this is due to Giovanni's three nearly equal stanzas (of first eight, then two six-line stanzas) consisting of enjambed lines that nonetheless seem to contain themselves line by line. The first stanza unfolds predictably as a series of statements, then reconsiderations, with the second pivoting on a near chiasmus—"of course you love me / but being loved of course"—that puts into question the logic of that reiterated "of course." By the third stanza, the poet at last acknowledges how little she shares the feelings of love her lover claims to feel for her, admitting that she is left "alone," "practicing / not having you to love."

This opening segment, which had begun with the painful concession of no longer being able to write, turns to a forlorn admission of no longer being able to love, as if the two conditions were
somehow intertwined. And the first stanza's professed unease in
writing (not having "written in so long") is matched by the third
stanza's admission that not having to love requires "practice" as
well. The very lack of punctuation itself reinforces a settled equiv-
alency in the poem's opening sequence—of writing versus love; of
love spelled out versus love simply present; of "you" and "i" forced
to shift uneasily back and forth in a fraught relationship—before
further stanzas establish the poet's achieved equilibrium: "but I
sit writing a poem / about my habits / which while it's not / a
great poem / is mine." Neither Cummings's whimsical play nor
Williams's searing attention to isolated words and their resonance
interest Giovanni, caught likewise in the creation of poems unmarked by punctuation that are meant nonetheless for investigat-
ing traditional humanistic subjects.

That intention is on full display in the title poem from her
1978 collection, "Cotton Candy on a Rainy Day" (*CP* 227–29),
which grew out of an experience with her nephew at the Cin-
cinnati Zoo. When a concession clerk officiously refused to sell
her cotton candy because the rain would melt it before it could
be enjoyed, Giovanni became infuriated. The idea of proscribing
indulgence because delight was evanescent seemed to her bizarre,
even inimical to any full-throated embrace of life itself (see Fowler, *Nikki* 88). And that feeling erupted in the meditation offered
through the long poem's four opening stanzas:

Don't look now
I'm fading away
Into the gray of my mornings
Or the blues of every night

Is it that my nails
  keep breaking
Or maybe the corn

on my second little piggy
Things keep popping out
on my face
  or
  of my life

It seems no matter how
I try I become more difficult
  to hold
I am not an easy woman
  to want

They have asked
  the psychiatrists   psychologists   politicians and
  social workers
What this decade will be
  known for
There is no doubt it is
  loneliness

The first stanza replaces punctuation with silently enjambed lines, confirming through the very absence of marks the fluid, indeterminate shape of first-person cotton candy melting in rain ("I'm fading away"). It is as if the lines themselves were somehow transformed into spun sugar, contemplating their own verbal melting. Still, the melting has only slightly distorted the stanza's overall shape and prosody, with two unbroken, unrhymed couplets askew by just a few feet as the opening spondaic beat slips first into an iambic, then an anapestic rhythm.

As well, however, the stanza can be read as expressing the poet's own emergent voice, trusting to a newfound willingness to embrace vaguely untoward possibilities, opening her up to less restrictive gendered and psychological realms. Moreover, the wonderful repetition of a long "a" sound through to the second stanza (echoing the dominant "rainy day" of the poem's title) somehow replaces the punctuational sequestering, from "fading away . . . gray . . . nails keep breaking / Or maybe." The sound is then suppressed for a stanza before reemerging in the "decade" of the fourth, and again "If loneliness were a grape" in the fifth. The absence of commas, periods, and dashes only encourages our subliminal desire for a punctuated sequence that might explain our loss, our change, our life's descent. Some assistance is provided by capitalization at the beginning of lines, with spaced pauses suggesting the possibility of separate sentences. Yet otherwise, nothing more than that long "a" sound reminds us of what we once were.

The second stanza confirms that the poet's body itself is changing, according to laws of physical decline that seem to anticipate as well a psychological toll. With the third, the poet fully confronts that toll, realizing how her efforts at love are stymied by an independent streak, playing out the conundrum of enjoying cotton candy as it melts in the rain. Still, an ambiguity lies at the heart of the stanza, sustained in part by its unpunctuated form, as she admits to making an effort to "try," though without indicating whether it is to try to become less difficult or become more independent. In any case, "more" is what occurs, with another's desire to "hold" her deflected by her own understandable changes, confounded by her lack of easy accessibility. The fourth stanza then turns to "They," an assorted group, who register how fully her personal sense of isolation has become a wider sociological condition. "Loneliness," in short, is recognizably the condition of life—of change, diminished powers, melting possibility, imaged figuratively in the "Cotton Candy / on a rainy day" that appears in the sixth, middle stanza of the poem. Throughout, the absence of punctuation reinforces the poem's exposure to a general, unconditional pressure from which we all succumb.

As the eighth stanza proclaims, "We all line up / at some midway point" in the general downward sweep, without the handrails and traffic signs that might help forestall further melting. Only in the tenth stanza are sound, space pauses, capitalization, and italics brought together, conjoined by the proudly proclaimed repetition of the titular strong "a" in "the same . . . STAY . . . *don't change baby don't / change*":

We are consumed by people who sing
   the same old song   STAY:
                      as sweet as you are
                      in my corner
Or perhaps   *just a little bit longer*
But whatever you do   *don't change baby baby don't*
   change

Amid the formal display of nearly melted cotton candy, itself stalwartly holding on, the poet resists that resistance, denies that ephemeral denial, and embraces the laws that sweep the diminishing present into a nostalgia-laden past. The very italicized phrases of this stanza register less an emphatic stress as punctuation than the fact that they are part of musical culture, the comforting bromides of lines from popular soul and R&B songs (see Fowler, *Nikki* 90; also Giovanni 417). And the space pauses that drive those lines to the far right of the page confirm the poet denying their implicit comfort, speaking instead for how fully desire possesses the other by demanding a life-denying lack of change, walling off consciousness against mutability.

The poem ends with something like a return to a more conventional (unmelted) form in two stanzas that confirm how little life can be understood by those willing to cling to permanence:

I strangle my words as easily as I do my tears
I stifle my screams as frequently as I flash my smile
  it means nothing
I am cotton candy on a rainy day
  the unrealized dream of an idea unborn

I share with the painters the desire
To put a three-dimensional picture
On a one-dimensional surface

The indented "it means nothing" comes as something of a surprise, as both apposition and entirely new statement, sliding the reader into the negligible naught of "I am cotton candy on a rainy day." We seem to have recovered from the apparent disarray of the tenth stanza, though only to prepare ourselves for another shower of rain and change. Curiously, the continuing absence of punctuation this late in the poem has little effect, since the end-stopped lines confirm at once the conviction of the poet in resisting change, and as well her own continuing uncertainty. Giovanni, like Cummings and Williams before her, seizes on the possibilities of punctuational guard rails removed, if only like them to reveal how words, spacing, and lines themselves can proclaim their own resonant if frequently unnoticed constraints.

8
Incarceration: Nabokov's Parentheses

Between the preceding discussion of writers who resist punctuation altogether, and the following investigation of an author who juggled an array of different marks, a glance at literary parentheses is in order if only briefly (parenthetically, as it were). No better instance presents itself than Vladimir Nabokov, who took self-conscious care to defend his manuscripts from ham-handed editors, fighting off prudent adjustments to his intemporate italicizations and moody ellipses. Yet the far more salient punctuation marking *Lolita* (1955) is its bountiful array of four hundred and fifty parentheses, which merge with a medley of other punctuational pauses to regularly arrest narrative motion. Just as regularly, they are meant to deflect attention from the narrator's revolting, indeed criminal, behavior in order to arouse appreciation for his stylish verbal facility; or as he intones at the opening: "You can always count on a murderer for a fancy prose style" (Nabokov, *Lo* 9). A personality at once various and contemptible, mesmerizing and abhorrent, lurks nearly everywhere through the calibrated punctuation of Humbert Humbert's confession, at once unmasked and painstakingly couched in pockets of artful prose.

But the most playfully calculated insights peep out not from proliferating commas or swiveling semicolons or sudden dashes, but from his surprisingly ubiquitous parenthetical interruptions. And that calculation often depends on reminding the reader of Humbert's present incarceration at the moment of writing, compounded by our subliminal awareness of a physical resemblance between brackets and bars. Actually penned in his prison cell, he seems in parenthetical asides to break through the fourth wall, reaching imaginatively across to us even as he alerts us to his actual confinement. "The bracket marks themselves serve as claustrophobic, typographical prisons of punctuation," Duncan White has observed; "as early as the second chapter, the reader is made aware of Humbert's jail cell: `nothing of her subsists within the hollows and dells of memory, over which, if you can stand my style (I am writing under observation), the sun of my infancy had set'" (White 52–53). And though the example is innocuous, White goes on to approve Craig Raine's (parenthetical) dismissal of "(Those vicious Nabokovian parentheses)" (Raine 323), concluding that the punctuational choice is always nefarious, decidedly "a symptom of Humbert's viciousness" (White 49). Or as he censoriously concludes: "Stylish cruelty is the hallmark of the Humbertian parenthesis" (White 50).

A closer look suggests something considerably more varied than sheer heartlessness in Humbert's parentheses, even as early as that "(I am writing under observation)," which Nabokov uses inventively to bring his fictional author imaginatively alive. Occasionally, Humbert injects monosyllabic descriptors to evoke a local reference, if only fleetingly. At one point, a "sleepy small town (elms, white church)" displays a postcard-ready, lightning-like blur of Norman Rockwell banality (Nabokov 35). Even earlier, he had filled in his own troubled history, again elliptically: "My very photogenic mother died in a freak accident (picnic, lightning) when I was three" (Nabokov, *Lo* 10), a gesture that White considers "typical of Humbert's flick-knife prose" (White 50).[1]

---

[1] Consider further White's charge:

> He regularly abuses his position of narratorial power, giving away glimpses of future developments: "A few words more about Mrs. Humbert while the going is good (a bad accident is to happen quite soon)" (79). Having already slipped in that he is a murderer, Humbert will keep providing further ambiguous clues. When Lolita is about to leave for Camp Q, Humbert drops another teasing clue; again in "casual" parenthesis: "My Lolita, who was half in and about to slam the car door, wind down the glass, wave to Louise and the poplars (whom and which she was never to see again) (66)" (White 59–60).

Yet the casual condensation of plot into minimal two-word constituents, though bloodless, reveals as well a rhetorical flair in a narrator we have just barely met—one whose parentheticals may appear offhand, even indifferent, but actually constitute a more calculated, manipulative shaping of narrative. Later, he will assess his suspected culpability for Charlotte Haze's accidental death in a similar if slightly more protracted series: "Within the intricacies of the pattern (hurrying housewife, slippery pavement, a pest of a dog, steep grade, big car, baboon at its wheel), I could dimly distinguish my own vile contribution" (Nabokov, *Lo* 103). Our sense of his cruelty, in short, is suitably leavened by wry admiration at his evocative narrative skill.[2]

More to the point, parentheses contribute to a range of emotional registers, including the enthusiasm with which he offers shout-outs to friends, prominently Jean Farlow: "'we may see each other again' (Jean, whatever, wherever you are, in minus time-space or plus soul-time, forgive me all this, parenthesis included)" (Nabokov, *Lo* 104–5). And his realization that the parenthesis relegates his avowal to something like auxiliary status is registered silently elsewhere: with "(hi, Ilse, you were a dear, uninquisitive soul, and you touched my dove very gently)"; or "(hi Rita—wherever you are, drunk or hangoverish, Rita, hi!)"; or "(Hi, Melmoth, thanks a lot, old fellow)" (Nabokov, *Lo* 198, 259, 307). With Humbert, we can never rest assured in the depth of his alleged feelings or purported intentions; after all, such exuberant acknowledgments may be genuinely felt, but they may also be easily and effectively feigned to mislead the reader into favoring him, disarmed by his dissembled high spirits. Either way, the

[2]Admittedly, Humbert's implacable ruthlessness is on occasion unmediated, as when Lolita comes into his room, noting "the hideous hieroglyphics (which she could not decipher) of my fatal lust" (Nabokov, *Lo* 48). More dramatically, Lo recognizes friends on the road at a mountain pass, "the backs of a family enjoying it (with Lo, in a hot, happy, wild, intense, hopeful, hopeless whisper—'Look the McCrystals, please let's talk to them, please'—let's talk to them, reader!—'please! I'll do anything you want, oh, please')" (Nabokov, *Lo* 157).

gestures are hardly cruel (in White's calculation), as Humbert recalls the Russian cab driver in Paris who stole his wife: "the good colonel (Maximovich! his name suddenly taxies back to me)" (Nabokov, *Lo* 30). The anthimeria of "taxies" coupled with the sudden recollected name exclaimed aloud alerts us to a spontaneously frisky Humbert, alive to the account he pens as we read.

Other occasions offer similar performative delights, reminding us that Humbert is ever attuned to his craft, misrecalling the name of an actor who "Appeared (I notice the slip of my pen in the preceding paragraph, but please do not correct it, Clarence)" (Nabokov, *Lo* 32). And in a later apologetic aside to that same lawyer from prison, he admits: "(this is not *too* clear I am afraid, Clarence, but I did not keep any notes)" (Nabokov, *Lo* 154). Occasionally, he simply throws up his hands: "that only a spell of insanity could ever give me the simple energy to be a brute (all this amended, perhaps)" (Nabokov, *Lo* 47). Such sundry gestures again have the playful effect of alerting us to Humbert writing in the present, living in the past, as if he were imaginatively soaring back and forth from a sequestering cell to the unending stratagems of memory, capable simultaneously of freedom and confinement: "I could be bounded in a nutshell, and count myself king of infinite space" (*Hamlet*, II. ii).

Yet the brackets that serve as "prisons of punctuation" for Humbert also tend to confine the reader into a series of presumed postures, all the while extending our amusement at his resourceful ways of surviving "the opaque air of this tombal jail" (Nabokov, *Lo* 109). When Lolita memorably (if only in memory) sits on his knee, he almost kisses her, but "I cannot tell my learned reader (whose eyebrows, I suspect, have by now traveled all the way to the back of his bald head), I cannot tell him how the knowledge came to me" (Nabokov, *Lo* 48). And that interruptive if stuttering repetition suggests how fully the parenthetical image of his invoked reader's shock has upset him. Much later, in a rare indirect invocation, he admits that "otherwise the reader (ah, if I could visualize him as a blond-bearded scholar with rosy lips sucking *la pomme de sa canne* as he quaffs my manuscript!) might not understand" (Nabokov, *Lo* 226). Parentheses work, in other words, to circumscribe both Humbert and the reader, as if we were both being bracketed into prescribed roles.

Throughout, excessive self-esteem alternates with an apparently troubled conscience in Humbert's parenthetical insertions, keeping us teeteringly aware of him as ever more than two-dimensional, always ready to shift gears and change directions should logic require. Even his claims for evidence supporting his narrative are apparently self-contradicted, as he admits of his preserved pocket diary: "Actually, it was destroyed five years ago and what we examine now (by courtesy of a photographic memory) is but its brief materialization" (Nabokov, *Lo* 40). A few pages later, however, in disregard of his earlier "Actually" and "brief," what appears to be the authentically physical chronicle magically reappears: "Only in the tritest of terms (diary resumed) can I describe Lo's features" (Nabokov, *Lo* 44). And as if further to confuse, he confesses of Charlotte's love letter to him that "What I present here is what I remember of the letter, and what I remember of the letter I remember verbatim (including that awful French). It was at least twice longer" (Nabokov, *Lo* 68).

By the end, amid seemingly muddled claims, we have grown thoroughly skeptical of this faultless, ambulatory camera-eye as he describes trying "in the remotest Northwest" to get a now married Lolita "'to leave your incidental Dick, and this awful hole, and come to live with me, and die with me, and everything with me' (words to that effect)" (Nabokov, *Lo* 4, 278). The more Humbert affirms the power of a "photographic memory," the less confident we become, especially given his otherwise stylish élan and narrative ingenuity. His pride in compositional skills, often registered as an aside, gradually makes us wonder at what is at stake in the telling: "The disappointment I must now register (as I gently grade my story into an expression of the continuous risk and dread that ran through my bliss) should in no wise reflect on the lyrical, epic, tragic but never Arcadian American wilds. They are beautiful, heart-rendingly beautiful, those wilds" (Nabokov, *Lo* 168).

Indeed, at various points, his gratified self-satisfaction blends with a deliberate skewering of English itself, as when his neighbor "barbered some late garden blooms or watered his car, or, at a later date, defrosted his driveway (I don't mind if these verbs are all wrong)" (Nabokov, *Lo* 179). And when last departing from pregnant Lolita, Humbert likewise shifts from the scene to its rhetorical effect in a punctuational hitch: "She and the dog saw me off. I was surprised (this is a rhetorical figure, I was not) that the sight of the old car in which she had ridden as a child and a nymphet, left her so very indifferent" (Nabokov 280). Still, in writing up the account months after, he admits to misleading those who might try to discover her and her husband "(. . . I have camouflaged everything, my love)"; he even disguises, with a parenthetical confession, their address as "let me see, 10 Killer Street (I am not going very far for my pseudonyms)" (Nabokov, *Lo* 267, 268).

But each of these slightly humorous, marginally cruel, overly self-conscious asides do not quite suggest the power of the many simply odd, often ironic observations inserted by the way. Consider when Humbert first views the Haze household, its interior itself become a metonymy for the possibilities represented by Lolita, "with limp wet things overhanging the dubious tub (the question mark of a hair inside)" (Nabokov, *Lo* 38). Later, in equally self-mocking moods, he first apologizes, "as if (to prolong these Proustian intonations)," and then complains: "this was the gesture ('look, Lord, at these chains!') that would have come nearest to the mute expression of my mood" (Nabokov, *Lo* 77, 83). Caught up in a passionate moment, he admits to a metathetic lapse: "'What's the katter with misses?' I muttered (word-control gone) into her hair" (Nabokov, *Lo* 120). And only moments after, he suffers "a fit of heartburn (they call those fries 'French,' *grand Dieu!*)" (Nabokov, *Lo* 129). Even a casual glance across western fields from their car provokes a whimsical excursus from Humbert: "there sometimes stood simple cows, immobilized in a position (tail left, white eyelashes right) cutting across all human rules of traffic" (Nabokov, *Lo* 153). Few other writers have ever used parentheses so chimerically, so evocatively, so mischievously as

Nabokov, as if he were testing the playful potential of a punctuational mark hitherto the tedious tool of footnoting sub-sub-librarians and finicky paralegals.

On that same automotive excursion, for instance, more soberly and hilariously, Humbert and Lolita "silently stared, with other motorists and their children, at some smashed, blood-bespattered car with a young woman's shoe in the ditch (Lo, as we drove on: 'That was the exact type of moccasin I was trying to describe to that jerk in the store')" (Nabokov, *Lo* 174). The conventional balustrade partitioning off the appalling from the ludicrous is typographically stamped, as so often in this novel, by the simplest of paired brackets, registering two exasperatingly different modes of feeling and thought. Humbert regularly pulls the reader out of one familiar emotional mode into another. In a more self-lacerating mode (suggested by an assumed nickname), Humbert turns his gimlet eye on himself, self-divided in a cross-examination about his abased demands of Lolita, posing as both interrogatee and interrogator: "Sometimes . . . Come on, how often exactly, Bert? Can you recall four, five, more such occasions? Or would no human heart have survived three? Sometimes (I have nothing to say in reply to your question)" (Nabokov, *Lo* 192, ellipsis in original). Again, rigid defensiveness needs to be quarantined in close proximity to the behavior that has generated it, unapologetically.

More generally, the point of so ample a review of Nabokov's parentheses is to reveal how they serve multiple, often conflicting purposes meant to engage the reader by the figure of Humbert as larger than life. Punctuation, in short, would seem to endorse him as charming, even charismatic, though those bracketed moments also help make him dangerously persuasive, revealing layers of emotional strife and intellectual friction that will never be resolved, but in their irresolution become endlessly entertaining. At such moments, it could be said he earns too much of our delighted interest, even sympathy, diverting attention from what is otherwise appalling in his behavior. And in that regard, parentheses become emblematic of the novel itself and its troubling oscillations.

Compounding their often wryly humorous, self-declaiming effect, parentheses offer Humbert a relentless way to enforce a callous control, allowing him to take delight in foreshadowing events that he obviously knows will occur (having already lived through them in his pre-confinement days). Invoking "Aubrey McFate (as I would like to dub that devil of mine)" (Nabokov, *Lo* 56), he corporealizes the ominousness that threads through much of his account, with brackets registering a supposed self-consciousness about doing so. Taking a fiercely anticipatory pride in the narrative power he exerts, he imagines Charlotte Haze's murder from a double perspective, one that luxuriates at once prospectively and retrospectively: "as I watched, with the stark lucidity of a future recollection (you know—trying to see things as you will remember having seen them)" (Nabokov, *Lo* 86). The point again, however, is that Nabokov's invocation of parentheses is otherwise multifaceted, making asides serve different, even contradictory ends.

For instance, on various occasions Humbert stops his narrative abruptly to allow a fuller, sometimes fantastical view of Lolita, as if to register how fully she has interrupted his own world even in imagined circumstances that hardly acquit him of the perversion he embraces so fully:

> And, as if I were the fairy-tale nurse of some little princess (lost, kidnaped [*sic*], discovered in gypsy rags through which her nakedness smiled at the king and his hounds), I recognized the tiny dark-brown mole on her side. With awe and delight (the king crying for joy, the trumpets blaring, the nurse drunk) I saw again her lovely indrawn abdomen where my southbound mouth had briefly paused, and those puerile hips. (Nabokov, *Lo* 39)[3]

---

[3]On the same page, another similar scene occurs, reinforcing the reader's mixed response:

> In the course of the sun-shot moment that my glance slithered over the kneeling child (her eyes blinking other those stern dark spectacles—the

But then, less fantastically if just as artfully, Humbert reads a list of her schoolmates, and breaks into Elizabethan tempos: "A poem, a poem, forsooth! So strange and sweet was it to discover this 'Haze, Dolores' (she!) in its special bower of names" (Nabokov, *Lo* 52). The shift from an earlier, shamelessly exploitative mode to this exclamatory delight in "(she!)" seems abrupt but no more so than all the mercurial moods traversed by Humbert. Occasionally, the object of his obsession even breaks into sentences as a two-letter expression of wonder ("Lo! . . . And behold" [Nabokov 51]), only to emerge parenthetically in her own person; a lower-case instance occurs unexpectedly when they drive past motels that "gradually form the caravansary, and, lo (she was not interested but the reader may be)" (Nabokov, *Lo* 210). Of course, the reader is always taken by Humbert's interpositions, as much for their content as for the accomplished, protean figure who maps them.

Of all the parenthetical interjections in the novel, however, one stands remarkably alone, appearing appropriately enough in the afterword penned by an author self-styled as "Vladimir Nabokov" (allegedly in his own voice). And this is the aside that conspicuously outlines his tersely expressed philosophy of art: "For me a work of fiction exists only insofar as it affords me what I shall bluntly call aesthetic bliss, that is a sense of being somehow, somewhere, connected with other states of being where art (curiosity, tenderness, kindness, ecstasy) is the norm" (Nabokov, *Lo* 314–15). The punctuation here does not quite wrap up narrative parentheses in the novel, though this occasion is its most pointed marking, signaling (as I have argued elsewhere) a vivid deflection from Humbert's prison-house preening through bracketing bars:

little Herr Doktor who was to cure me of all my aches) while I passed by her in my adult disguise (a great big handsome hunk of movieland manhood), the vacuum of my soul managed to suck in every detail of her bright beauty, and these I checked against the features of my dead bride. (Nabokov 39)

That sequence of four descriptive nouns entered parenthetically ("curiosity, tenderness, kindness, ecstasy") offers a curious re-introduction of the ethical back into the novel, and in so doing establishes the terms by which a reading of Humbert should be pursued. After all, kindness, curiosity and tenderness are the very virtues he lacks in his narcissistic subjugation of Lolita—a subjugation we eerily reinforce in our own delight at his dazzling verbal skill. But as well, consider how the first three nouns (all ethical) require prepositions, involving others—curiosity *about*, tenderness *towards*, kindness *for*—while ecstasy is something that can be achieved alone, requiring neither preposition nor an ethical component. (Mitchell, *More* 115)

Like Humbert, Nabokov can be a slippery figure prone to slyly equivocal claims, though here he offers a staunch elucidation meant as indictment of his main character, not endorsement. And it is appropriate that he inserts it as parenthetical extension in a novel where parentheses never seem amiss, however various their effects.

Returning to Humbert Humbert, we realize how fully his self-revelations also occur in parentheses, though more often in sportively mocking tones than in candid self-appraisal. His hesitant, unreliable claims to remorse seem compressed most vividly, typographically, with his unregenerate lust. It is there, in the exposed prison bars of that particular form of punctuation, that we are reminded of Humbert's arrant desire still peeking through his self-serving claims of moral transformation and remorse. Every time parenthetical marks appear, we are reminded of his exclusions, his unaccountable jumps of memory, his bipolar compulsions, and the uses of irony he masters so transfiguringly into a double-edged rhetorical sword.

9

Plenitude: Faulkner's Array

Few other prose writers have had so deft an understanding of the power of suppressed punctuation as Faulkner, apparent in his embrace for extended stretches *in prose* of the absence of any punctuation at all. More generally, he is unsurpassed in self-consciousness about the swerves of language, in all its verbal disruptions and rhythmic fluctuations. Clearly, he grasped how fully punctuational marks—and all the other iconographic gestures, ligatures, signs, and spacings—succeed not simply in guiding expression but in actually creating meaning. Nor did he limit himself to single options, self-consciously inserting both idiosyncratic graphic figures and odd poetic spaces in his fictions, presenting us with nonverbal shapes and physical images, interspersing his narrative lines with a mixed cocktail of punctuation marks, and marks combined and commingled (parentheses *within* parentheses and dashes that pause prose for pages at a time): all as a means of reminding the reader of what diction by itself both actually accomplishes and where it can founder. For all its variety, however, his prose experiments track a certain pattern that leads from early minimalism to a later inclination toward amalgamated (and complicated) punctuational matches.

Start with his early story "A Rose for Emily" (1930) in which he relies on dashes as thoroughly as James: thirty-five times in only nine pages, accompanied by two parentheses. What does that unusual accumulation achieve? Or perhaps more productively, what do such frequent dashes in this narrative context presume, especially given how little Faulkner relies on them (at least exclusively) in later fictional explorations? Part of the effect has to do with the

retrospective nature of the narrative, circling back from its opening "When Miss Emily Grierson died" through a shuttered biography of her, to the moment immediately after the funeral when
the town discovers the mummified corpse of a poisoned lover in
her bed (Faulkner, "Rose" 47). We realize that Emily's reclusive
antipathy to change itself, stalwartly denying time's effects, is reflected in the narrative, in her resistance to burying her father,
to paying taxes, to acknowledging peoples' deaths, to accepting
temporal transition of any kind. Yet the narrator repeatedly registers through adverbial clauses her immersion *in time*, effectively
celebrating while at the same time ruefully exposing her history
as a figure of staunch resistance to Northern aggression.

That persistent, dominant rhythm posing Emily against
temporal sequence is configured, and strangely compounded,
through the em dashes Faulkner adopts. Dashes more than occasionally slow the narrative pace, as if confirming the story's
plot, and do so self-consciously as an all but visual cue. After her
father's death, Emily is described as physically transformed, yet
having "a vague resemblance to those angels in colored church
windows—sort of tragic and serene" (Faulkner, "Rose" 52). Later,
Homer Barron appears, and the town wonders at his attraction,
especially since "Homer himself had remarked—he liked men,
and it was known that he drank with the younger men . . . —
that he was not a marrying man" (Faulkner, "Rose" 55). Or when
the town rebels against her dalliance, "at last the ladies forced the
Baptist minister—Miss Emily's people were Episcopal—to call
upon her" (Faulkner, "Rose" 55).

In a narrative so calculatedly oriented to reversing the effects
of time, with Emily's death announced at the outset only to be
delayed until the end, and with Emily herself tenaciously opposed
to any transition or variation, it is as if her spirit were somehow
emblematized by em dashes. Her energy is as abrupt as the marks
that brake the pace of the chorus-narrator's patter so as to define
a more intrepid allegiance to the past. And ironically, her death
at last achieves for both town and reader precisely the suspension
of time that she had striven to achieve throughout (configured in

the absence of dashes, all but one set, in the story's final section once she is dead).

In the same year, *As I Lay Dying* (1930) offered a fuller test that variously advanced on Faulkner's break-through novel, *The Sound and the Fury* (1929), in which punctuation had already been disrupted giving voice to the three acutely aggrieved Compson brothers. Both novels toyed with augmented possibilities of italics as a displaced form of punctuation, invoking the font in the earlier novel as rough marker for shifts in time (in Benjy's ever-present section) or to register fluctuations in consciousness (in Quentin's desperately psychopathological section).[1] But Darl Bundren's gift of clairvoyance in *As I Lay Dying* forms something of a punctuational leap, with impossibly far-flung or otherwise clandestine events represented in roman type, coupled with a shift into italics that evokes circumstances available to normal sensory contact.[2] As well, Faulkner flirts with other italic possibilities in monologues by Dewey Dell and Vardaman as well as Vernon Tull, alerting the reader to apparent revelations, or unacknowledged self-divisions, or competing internal voices.[3] In each case, a distinct punctuational meaning needs to be actively interpreted rather than simply read out as either pause or digression.

As well, Faulkner registers an odd marking of ellipses in the novel, using seven periods rather than the customary three, making us wonder what is conveyed by extending the conventional series (a habit that continues in *Absalom, Absalom!*). Is it to suggest typographically that the omitted sequence of words or

[1]Since James's dictation of punctuation has been addressed earlier, it is worth noting that Faulkner's handwritten pages for the novel were quite precise in indicating italicization with underlinings, confirmed by this manuscript page from the "Digital Yoknapatawpha" collection: http://faulkner.iath.virginia.edu/media/resources/MANUSCRIPTS/AILDMS14.html

[2]But see different use of italics for Darl (Faulkner, *AILD* 147–48, 180–83, 213).

[3]See for Dewey Dell (Faulkner, *AILD* 121); for Vardaman (Faulkner, *AILD* 151, 194–96, 215 [with italics but no periods], 223, 225, 249–520); and for Vernon Tull (Faulkner, *AILD* 90–92).

even sheer time itself is greater than we might typically imagine? Then why not vary the number of periods to adjust each breach appropriately?[4] A more obvious temporal explanation occurs for the insertion of actual spaces between words, sometimes as physical emblems of silence in the recurrent "Chuck chuck chuck " of Cash's adze, or as visual epitomes in Addie Bundren's description of her body before her family began, where she "used to be a virgin" (Faulkner, *AILD* 5, 173).

At other moments, Faulkner surprises the reader with a vivid absence of periods, when instead of signaling a sentence's closure punctuation is simply removed, leaving us to wonder why. In Vardaman's sections, this reflects little more than his loose grasp of events (and proper grammar). But in Dewey Dell's third section, it occurs abruptly and more significantly, as she now is notably pregnant and no longer suffering menses. Of Cash's five sections, two end in mid-sentence (the only ones in the novel to do so), with an absence of periods leading to ambiguous possibilities: the first, that he has proved so unimaginative and predictable that we can presume what he is about to say, as sheer run-on continuation of his mildly obsessed trains of thought; the second, that he actively exceeds the meanings suggested by his monologue, as if he were actually more expansive and self-sufficient than his dull words might otherwise intimate.

[4]John Lennard has pointed to Harold Pinter's variously dotted pauses in *The Caretaker* (1960): "Pinter's four-dot pauses are usually terminal, and appear to compromise the conventional number of suspension marks and a period; but the use of a five-dot and many three-dot pauses in Aston's long speech ending Act II can only be interpreted as registering the different duration of different silences" (Lennard 285, note 24). For an intriguing investigation of Ralph Ellison's racialized use of ellipses in *Invisible Man* (1952), see Jennifer DeVere Brody, who claims "the ellipsis is ambivalent, enigmatic, paradoxical—the presence of absence (or vice versa) that like the blackness of blackness both 'is and aint'" (Brody 73). Or as she reiterates: "The blackness of blackness is both textual and performative—figured as, in, and by—the ellipsis" (Brody 74). As well, see Fredson Bowers on "normalizing" ellipses (Bowers 94–95).

By contrast to spaces and periods, invoked so resourcefully throughout, only one parenthesis occurs in the entire novel, appropriately in Darl's section as part of a precise depiction, with the bracketed insertion revealing a further dimension to his circumspect eye: "The wagon is hauled clear, the wheels chocked (carefully: we all helped; it is as though upon the shabby, familiar, inert shape of the wagon there lingered somehow, latent yet still immediate, that violence which had slain the mules that drew it not an hour since) above the edge of the flood" (Faulkner, *AILD* 157). Of course, the precision here is again akilter, part of the same psychological dissonance revealed in the dismayingly long mental turmoil sandwiched between Anse's early question on one page, "Where's Jewel?" and Darl's terse response more than a page later, "Down to the barn" (Faulkner, *AILD* 10–11). Darl's inability to subordinate needless verbiage from essential facts is so fundamental a part of his psychology that paradoxically what might seem to be the appropriate punctuation for untangling his psychology (parentheses) cannot be invoked without misrepresenting that psychology, in his unwavering inability to subordinate. Notably, moreover, though Faulkner earlier relied heavily on dashes in stories, rarely does he turn to them in his early novels despite sliding into nearly every other form of punctuation.[5]

The sense one gains, especially as evoked in Faulkner's later works, is that consciousness is not so much broken into or otherwise sharply disrupted as it is shaped, molded, swayed, slipped from one accessed corner to another.[6] And *Absalom, Absalom!* finally explores most forcefully and ingeniously the potential of

[5]André Bleikasten has observed that "the suppression of punctuation not only breaks up syntactic relationships but tends to annul them. In Dewey Dell's account of her dream (115–16), as in Vardaman's relation of the river crossing (143–44), it leads to a leveling process in which words are reduced to a sort of verbal magma" (Bleikasten 33).

[6]In 1956, Faulkner claimed he "tried to crowd and cram everything, all experience, into each paragraph, to get the whole complete nuance of the moment's experience, of all the recaptured light rays" (Faulkner, *Lion* 107). For a survey of critiques of Faulkner's late style, see Eric Sandarg (34–6).

punctuation pressed to the limits. This first occurs in the initial account of the scene that forms the novel's center, as a mystified Quentin Compson tries to make sense of Rosa Coldfield's outraged account:

> —the two separate Quentins now talking to one another in the long silence of notpeople in notlanguage, like this: *It seems that this demon—his name was Sutpen—(Colonel Sutpen)—Colonel Sutpen. Who came out of nowhere and without warning upon the land with a band of strange niggers and built a plantation— (Tore violently a plantation, Miss Rosa Coldfield says)—tore violently. And married her sister Ellen and begot a son and a daughter which—(Without gentleness begot, Miss Rosa Coldfield says)—without gentleness. Which should have been the jewels of his pride and the shield and comfort of his old age, only—(Only they destroyed him or something or he destroyed them or something. And died)—and died. Without regret, Miss Rosa Coldfield says—(Save by her) Yes, save by her. (And by Quentin Compson) Yes. And by Quentin Compson.* (Faulkner, *Absalom* 4–5)

This lightning flash of revelation encapsulates the entire novel, though at this early point it is hardly apparent what the flash might actually mean. Hereafter, the scene will be repeatedly glossed, distended, embroidered, unfolded, and filled in. Yet here, the alteration of italic (recollected time) and roman (present time); the syntactical disruption of so many dashes; the appositions, repetitions, and Rosa's overzealous corrections, signaled by parentheses; even the unruly periods that mark off not complete sentences so much as disconnected outbursts: all figure forth at once the disarray of the past in its urgency and violence, and the incomprehension of the present in the face of such an inaugural outburst.

Quentin's dismay vividly matches our own at this juncture, though names, events, and unbridled passions (all unraveled in the novel to follow) are less compelling than the punctuational explosion that leaves us figuratively blistered and mentally riven. Even the strange compound words, collapsing nouns into their own negation, present a series of miniature versions of the tableau vivant revealed more generally here in its first visual form.[7] And the center of this subjective confusion occurs when Quentin overtakes Rosa's hortatory correctives to unmask his own dismayed incomprehension: "*only—(Only they destroyed him or something or he destroyed them or something. And died)—and died*" (Faulkner, *Absalom* 5). Finally, amid the jungle gym of punctuation, their two voices intertwine, with Rosa confirming Quentin's central role as if displacing her own, with punctuation confirming the narrating reversal at work. This would seem as important as the accumulated, barely understood narrative itself, attempting to weave together a history that might actually, adequately explain the brutal murder of a brother.

Perhaps more saliently, however, is the way revelation and obscurity are yoked together through punctuation that folds the

---

[7]For a brilliant reading of Faulkner's unpunctuated "adjectival chains," beginning with the novel's opening words—"From a little after two oclock until almost sundown of the long still hot weary dead September afternoon they sat" (Faulkner, *Absalom* 3)—see Garrett Stewart (111–13). As John Tamplin has observed:

Faulkner uses this technique of stacking adjectives without any conjunctions, and he has developed it since *Light in August*. The adjectives all modify the same thing—they delay the nomination of that thing—they give ample time to the expression of many aspects of the thing—they correct each other, or add layers and reduce misinterpretations possible from those that precede. This technique is a miniature, word-level version of what Faulkner is up to in the rest of the novel—recurring images that only gradually come into focus. The interesting thing about this technique is that it opens the possibility of its own infinite continuation. Faulkner shows that truth can't be reached from one perspective, by misleading us with each perspective in isolation from the rest. But this doesn't entail that there is a certain number of perspectives that, once expressed, will reach the absolute truth of the matter. Faulkner's technique questions the possibility of a truth, even in his choice of adjectives. (Tamplin)

For an account of compound words in Faulkner, see BLD in MT and Clifford Wulfman.

passage repetitively back on itself. It is as if, in his most magisterial narrative, delving so ambitiously into the social ravages of racism, slavery, and the historical debacle of the Civil War, Faulkner could only weave his tormented account together through an equally tormented syntax. And his complicated mélange of dashes, semi-colons, colons, italics, self-negating neologisms, parentheses (and parentheses within) all serve as a means of foregrounding not simply the uncertainty of what is being described, or its mutual negotiation and confluence of multiple voices, but also the meta-textuality of the whole—the fact that punctuation serves here less to match oral evocation than to clarify how fully the evocations are in fact being written, imagined, indeed self-consciously distanced from the scene they are transparently supposed to evoke.[8]

The novel's first half shifts between Rosa's impassioned outbursts at an experience that has undone her (in chapters 1 and 5) and Mr. Compson's tight-lipped, primly judicious accounting (in chapters 2–4), inquiring into a past he self-admittedly fails to understand. Accordingly, his three sections are dominated by periods, sometimes dashes, occasionally commas, all suggesting something of the deliberate, quietly balanced tone of his report. Only with Rosa's second section do we at last get a profound sense of the effect produced by her inimitable voice: angry, outraged, unappeased after a half-century of rejection obsessively remembered with fuller knowledge of the cause of it all perpetually deferred. And the entire account occurs italicized, as if to register the contrast between her own inordinately impassioned tone and Mr. Compson's matter-of-fact restraint. But as well, her voice is represented through the back-stepping, circling, self-interrupting rhythm of all the punctuational pauses we have reviewed up to now. Consider her remarkable lyric peroration, which begins

[8]As Eric Sandarg observes of Faulkner's use of parentheses: "By prolonging the action, Faulkner creates a significant level of suspense—but at the risk of confusing a likely already frustrated reader" (Sandarg 47). See as well Sandarg's useful distinction between the "periodic sentence" and the "cumulative sentence" (Sandarg 47–49).

with a sharply dashed aposiopesis, unexpectedly interrupting herself before she has truly begun:

> *Once there was—Do you mark how the wistaria, sun-impacted on this wall here, distills and penetrates this room as though (light-unimpeded) by secret and attritive progress from mote to mote of obscurity's myriad components? That is the substance of remembering—sense, sight, smell: the muscles with which we see and hear and feel—not mind, not thought: there is no such thing as memory: the brain recalls just what the muscles grope for: no more, no less: and its resultant sum is usually incorrect and false and worthy only of the name of dream.—See how the sleeping outflung hand, touching the bedside candle, remembers pain, springs back and free while mind and brain sleep on and only make of this adjacent heat some trashy myth of reality's escape: or that same sleeping hand, in sensuous marriage with some dulcet surface, is transformed by that same sleeping brain and mind into that same figment-stuff warped out of all experience. Ay, grief goes, fades; we know that—but ask the tear ducts if they have forgotten how to weep.—Once there was (they cannot have told you this either) a summer of wistaria.* (Faulkner, *Absalom* 115)

The sentences appear to move as readily backward as forward, defying narrative (even descriptive) sequence and refusing a cumulative understanding.

Indeed, the flow of syntax seems distinctively oral, though the alternation of questions and answers, the development of what seems like an argument for memory and sense, is all propelled by dashes, commas, and sequential colons that reverse an onward flow: settling on a semantics that attempts to capture memory with its distortions; to register bodily pain as analogy and transformation. She begins with "*Once there was—*" as a gesture that immediately derails into a consideration of the powers of memory itself, though she does not return to the "*was*" of that preamble, instead simply denying the existence of any "*such thing as memory.*" All we have, as Rosa's account of Sutpen will attest, are "*incorrect*" images that have the ligatured framing of a dream. And finally Rosa returns to repeat her now-stuttering overture, having moved us closer to the past not at all.

Anger so fiercely sustained only succeeds in infusing Rosa's voice with a densely poetic, evocative inflection, since though it is directed outward at that "*fiend blackguard and devil*" (Faulkner, *Absalom* 10), it also turns inward, making her more self-conscious, self-expressive, and finally as central a figure in her account as Sutpen is to the story she otherwise wants to be told. Sounding like someone at once deranged yet perfectly in tune with her feelings, she fiercely pushes the limits of sensation and experience. That is, in her interrogation of the past, Rosa extolls the possibility of memory even as she defies its power, as if the experience that induced such anguish had somehow disappeared, leaked away. Memory takes on a life of its own, somehow losing connection with the very experience that sets it in motion. The body feels pain, willy-nilly, and seems unable to forget that feeling forty-odd years later, only kept alive by her own anguished voice. Reinforcing that memory in this summer of 1909 is the blooming wisteria evoking that scent-laden summer of a half-century before. Referents here seem unstable, but the meaning seems more or less clear: that just as wisteria distills through a room, particulate "mote to mote" in sheer permeating diffusion, so the body recalls its past. A sleeping mind transforms pain into an acceptable fiction (via a dream) but the body always refuses such fictions ("*ask the tear ducts if they have forgotten how to weep*").

Yet the striking aspect of the passage, like the rest of her section, hinges on Rosa's self-interruptions: the dashes that puncture the onward flow of memory and contemplation; the parenthesis that contributes an unneeded detail; then the sequence of clauses divided by colons that erupt four times before the sentence is brought to a halt. Immediately, a dash occurs that seems again unnecessary except to further break the flow. The whole defies coherent sequence, confirming how fully her life has for decades consisted of bodily pain, grief regularly dying back only to erupt again, sleep rudely interrupted, the redolent smell of wistaria then and now. And again, it is bare punctuation that evokes this state, especially in Faulkner's defiance of conventional usage. Take simply his abundant parentheses, as Fred D. Randel has duly counted: "*Absalom, Absalom!* pays little heed to the voice of common sense on the parenthesis. In the three hundred seventy-two pages . . . Faulkner uses . . . five hundred ninety-four parentheses or an average of 1.6 per page. They range in length from one word to several pages" (Randel 71).

Greater interest than sheer numbers, however, lies in the way parentheses become more intricate and confounding through the latter part of the novel. Rosa's central section tends to invoke parentheses as reminders ("so they will tell you" [107]) or as obsessive reiterations (say, of Sutpen's various brutalities), but they do not fundamentally disorient the reader. By the opening of Chapter 6, however, parentheses spread their compassing curves for a more complicated verbal embrace, after the section opens in Cambridge with italicized lines from Mr. Compson's January letter informing Quentin of Rosa's death. Precipitously, that moment is then interrupted by roman type reminding us of "that very September evening itself" months earlier, with Quentin's irritated thoughts in open parenthesis—"(and he soon needing, required, to say 'No, neither aunt cousin nor uncle Rosa . . .'"—as contested domains of Quentin's consciousness are revealed.

The novel indiscriminately mingles italics and roman, direct and indirect discourse, importuning demand and calm description, only finally to end with a closed parenthesis that momentarily seems to contain the mental upheaval, followed by a temporal repetition: "*Why do they live at all)*—that very September evening when Mr Compson stopped talking at last" (Faulkner, *Absalom* 142). A page later, Quentin's Harvard roommate interrupts, his exuberance bubbling over in a fashion that only spurs Quentin further—"(then Shreve again, 'Wait. Wait. You mean that this old gal, this Aunt Rosa—'" [Faulkner, *Absalom* 143])—this time however with the absence of any matching closing parenthesis itself. That absence seems to announce how fully Shreve McCannon's prodding to recall, rethink, recount, as well as his repetition of Quentin's words, will animate the rest of the novel.

Subsequent passages cordoned off by parentheses seem to grow ever longer, as if thoughts generated by the narrative simply exfoliated—even as italics take over (from pp. 148–52 entirely) to suggest how much alternative thinking is occurring. Even then, we return once again to another of Shreve's parenthetical questions about Judith following Sutpen's death: ("—'How was it?' Shreve said. 'You told me; how was it?'" [Faulkner, *Absalom* 152]). And the very deferral of closure to that parenthetical opening query suggests again how entirely an answer puzzlingly eludes them both. Two chapters later, near the end of the novel, a kind of resolution ensues in the return at last to Mr. Compson's letter, once again in italics.

The novel's final three sections become at once clearer and more embrangled, as Quentin and Shreve elucidate the mystery of why Henry murdered Bon at Sutpen's front gate amid punctuation that continues to tighten even as the flow paradoxically seems less interrupted. It is as if the rhythm here defies the cumulative, woodenly progressive pacing of Mr. Compson's rational narrative by contributing a more sequential (if broken) pattern in accessing the past. Simply by pausing to dilate and expatiate (with dashes, parentheses, and colons) that rhythm highlights the caution required in entering a realm that can never be categorically known:

> They stared—glared—at one another, their voices (it was Shreve speaking, though save for the slight difference which the intervening degrees of latitude had inculcated in them (differences not in tone or pitch but of turns of phrase and usage of words), it might have been either of them and was in a sense both: both thinking as one, the voice which happened to be speaking the thought only the thinking become audible, vocal; the two of them creating between them, out of the rag-tag and bob-ends of old tales and talking, people who perhaps had never existed at all anywhere, who, shadows,

were shadows not of flesh and blood which had lived and died but shadows in turn of what were (to one of them at least, to Shreve) shades too) quiet as the visible murmur of their vaporising breath. The chimes now began to ring for midnight. (Faulkner, *Absalom* 243)

Here, the initial reversal of dashes moderates immediately, while parentheses quietly insert themselves (even within other parentheses, sometimes left unclosed, as if in gentle accommodation to obscure, even simply imagined recesses of the past).[9] As well, commas, colons, and semicolons urge a depiction of the Harvard roommates aligning themselves with the story they want told, but doing so divergingly, in measured steps along forking paths. The tentative quality of the punctuation itself, set in roman type, confirms a quality of intelligent, nimble curiosity altogether different from Rosa's anguished account or Mr. Compson's calm rationale.

The power of that active, shaping curiosity is signaled some pages later in much the same way, when Shreve hypothesizes how Bon must have been devastated by Sutpen's refusal to send for him: "And maybe he didn't even say then, 'But he sent no word to me?'" (Faulkner, *Absalom* 267). Here again the punctuation shifts with Shreve's mental adjustment, as he and Quentin explore the possible narrative swerves that could adequately explain the murderous standoff at the gates of Sutpen's Hundred. And the very repetitions help confirm the need for tentativeness, carefully easing up on their joint assessment as they align ("not two but four of them") in imaginative partnership with the figures they so want to understand.

[9]Michelle Denham has claimed, "For Virginia Woolf's *To The Lighthouse*, the parenthesis works as a way of presenting simultaneity of experiences when spatially separated. For William Faulkner's *Absalom, Absalom*, the parenthesis creates a kind of compressed time, so that the past becomes a heavy burden upon the present, as represented by the way a narrative experience can be extended within parentheses" (Denham Abstract). For the best scholarly study of the emergence and use of parentheses, see John Lennard *passim*.

Shreve ceased. That is, for all the two of them, Shreve and Quentin, knew he had stopped, since for all the two of them knew he had never begun, since it did not matter (and possibly neither of them conscious of the distinction) which one had been doing the talking. So that now it was not two but four of them riding the two horses through the dark over the frozen December ruts of that Christmas eve: four of them and then just two—Charles-Shreve and Quentin-Henry, the two of them both believing that Henry was thinking *He* (meaning his father) *has destroyed us all,* not for one moment thinking *He* (meaning Bon) *must have known or at least suspected this all the time; that's why he has acted as he has, why he did not answer my letters last summer nor write to Judith, why he has never asked her to marry him;* believing that that must have occurred to Henry. (Faulkner, *Absalom* 267)

There are other moments of joint invention that are more distressing, more confusing, more precarious, but this nicely captures how central Faulkner's intricately mapped punctuation becomes.

Again, the experimentation in earlier narratives with different insertions, pauses, and italicizings has merged in the effort to reveal Quentin's and Shreve's collaboration in their ever uncertain enterprise. They actively create the past, through sympathy and invention, but the necessary frailty of their endeavor itself is enacted in the narrative's own repetitions, appositions, and reversals. And the disruptive parenthetical identifications have the paradoxical effect of keeping us slightly off balance, alert to alternative possibilities, as if conjoined intellectually with the roommates' efforts, far more than we would be without them. As the last two sections float into and out of italics, we grasp how fully the two freshmen themselves are meant to be understood as floating into and out of the past they invent.

In the midst of *Absalom, Absalom!*, we come to realize that its use of all the differing categories of punctuation becomes a means of foregrounding the narrative's own textuality. Pointedly, it highlights those uncertain contingencies and baffling enigmas obscured by any confident resting on unadorned fact. What might otherwise consist of simple presentation—of character, event, or mood—becomes through punctuational pauses, emphases, divergences, and reversals an entirely transformed set of mental negotiations as voices conflict with themselves, and unconscious thoughts and feelings erupt to the reader's uncertain dismay. Perhaps the point is just to remind us of the novel's opening claim, that Quentin's "very body was an empty hall echoing with sonorous defeated names; he was not a being, an entity, he was a commonwealth" (Faulkner, Absalom 7). And for Faulkner, deft punctuation assures that those "defeated names" will find effective expression in that democratic "commonwealth" of past and present. Throughout (to shift the analogy, if abruptly), typographical marks operate like the automotive transmission implicitly imagined by Adorno, contributing through characteristic configurations a sharply braking, abruptly U-turning, sometimes simply soft-pumping insistence to the ongoing flow of temporal narrative.

Epilogue: Punctuation as Style

Clearly, authors differ wildly from each other—indeed, differ from their earlier selves—in the ways they wield syntax for a desired end. They stall time, bending and wrapping it back on itself, delaying action, pausing, summarizing in all the ways pacing allows, even as they find other means of sparking narrative advances, lunging forward, keeping momentum sustained and sometimes impelled.[1] As importantly, authors notably seize on particular, sometimes favored typographical means of defining consciousness, revealing mixed understandings, sudden reservations, abrupt about-faces, or simply gentle divagations via punctuation that silently promotes such effects. And much as character and event are altered in the signature prose expressions invoked by different authors, so too is expression altered by the rhythms in which it unfolds. Like actual landscape itself, which offers up topoi we recognize in the rocky synclines and horticultural prospects that differ region by region, creating identifiable vistas, so textual landscapes become easily identifiable, shaped by punctuation that looms far more importantly than geography in any reading of fiction that truly moves us. As Garrett Stewart reminds us, proclaiming punctuation as style's unsung hero: "If syntax is the armature of prose and poetic form, along with enjambment in the latter, punctuation is an active part of the infrastructure in each case: the visible bolts and nuts, latches and hinges, of grammar's manifestation in literary pace and emphasis" (Stewart, private correspondence).

Of course, assessments above have only hinted at the range of available punctuational effects. Little has been said, for exam-

---

[1] For the single best scholarly assessment of this issue, see Brian Gingrich.

ple, of exclamation points (save for Poe's hysterical short story), though few other marks draw such instant attention to what is being expressed. F. Scott Fitzgerald once called for authors to "[c]ut out all these exclamation points," explaining that "[a]n exclamation point is like laughing at your own joke" (Kunsa 146). And Elmore Leonard, following Mary Oliver's frugal vision of punctuation, has notoriously offered a rule against any such indulgence: "You are allowed no more than two or three per 100,000 words of prose." But as Ben Blatt has noticed, even Leonard failed this rule in over forty novels "totaling 3.4 million words. If he had followed his own advice, he would have used only 102 exclamation points in his entire career. In practice, he used 1,651. That's 16 times as many as he recommended!" (Blatt). Even Blatt concedes, however, that Leonard was a lightweight where exclamation points were concerned, defeated by James Joyce with some 1,105 uses in only three novels.[2]

Despite such reliance on a sometimes abused punctuation mark, no one would presume to claim that either Leonard or Joyce are defined by the choice, far less that it expressed a "signature" style. Joy Williams, on the other hand, does notably succeed through a variety of stories in transforming sheer disjointedness into narrative delight through mere exclamation, "with deadpan pronouncements erupting cheek by jowl amid mundane events, often set off by an uncommonly loose splash of exclamation points" (Mitchell, *Mere* 115). Her preference for such spiked delights offers a sense of wonder at the strangeness of her often liminal, uncanny, even supernatural and spectral worlds. An exclamatory punctuation mark attests to her strange sense of life lived at an angle askew from common sense, where understanding breaks down and sheer untoward experience becomes commonplace.

---

[2]Though it is still worth a look at this site: "Welcome to the blog that exists to chronicle the excessive and unnecessary use of exclamation points we see in the every day world! Send your submissions to http://excessiveexclamation.blogspo t.ca/"

Then again, what do we make of moments where punctuation suggests not surprise or wonder, but absence and bewilderment? What, in other words, of things left out of account (themselves marked, once again, by present punctuation itself)? Ellipses serve to sever dramatic moments through a breach in continuity, shading off from emotional entanglement and moving us along as readers through a transpositional gesture. First here, then there, without the sly, trembling, irritated evocations that accompany our usual waking hours. That seems to be the takeaway of an ellipsis contrasted with a period, much less the possibilities (so far, unregistered) of a contrast with a colon. Further, what of punctuation used against the grammatical grain, in the infractions of comma splices and sentence fragments, where the common default of supposed sloppiness is turned somehow purposeful.

But instead of turning backward to venues unexplored, it may be worth directing our attention forwards to punctuational possibilities converted and transformed by new social media. The rejection of periods in the internet age has already been discussed, but what of other forms of punctuation, including emojis and hashtags? Jeff Scheible has traversed much of this territory, allowing that

> identifying such a mark as punctuation, when it has not traditionally been used in writing as punctuation, productively alerts us to shifts in the ways language and image relate to each other via contemporary textual practices. Perhaps the most illustrative and familiar example of this is writing emoticons, where iconic compositions of punctuation integrated within textual exchanges call attention to new configurations and alliances between language and image within social practices, mirroring and standing in for a broader shift that has occurred with the emergence of digital media cultures. (Scheible 3–4)[3]

---

[3]For fuller discussion of "the linguistics of emoji" and their "gestural" quality, see Gretchen McCulloch, Ch. 5: "Emoji and Other Internet Gestures" (McCulloch 155–95).

These "shifts" lay bare, as Marquard Smith has provocatively claimed, that in our current moment, "all content has become largely irrelevant. What matters," he writes, "is not *what* is gathered, arranged, and transmitted, but *how* such gathering, arranging, and transmitting works. 'What' is supplanted by 'how'" (Smith 385). From this perspective, typographical markers (emojis, digital icons) might seem to have outflanked lexemic signifiers (words strung together in sentences), which have for centuries formed the semantic basis of social communication. But any transition to the overpowering role of punctuational ploys seems true only in the admittedly very different realms of social media.

From a longer perspective, it is clear that punctuation actually subsists on words, and matters only because of them. If nothing else, this book is meant to convey how fully a generous symbiosis exists between marks of punctuation and the specific diction they divert, like sheepdogs managing—sometimes gently, sometimes not—a flock. Many of the most distinguished efforts of human expression occur in ineffable prose and poetry, and those efforts exist as much in the resonances evoked by unexpected words as in the suasions induced by unforeseen typographical marks. But only by weighing the pressures of punctuation against the syntax controlled by it (or, conversely, ignored) can we begin to explain the magic we feel in the process of simply scanning a page: our reading selves figuratively altered by the altering of marks themselves.

Bibliography

Adorno, Theodor W. "Punctuation Marks" (1956). *The Antioch Review* 48.3, Poetry Today (Summer, 1990): 300–5.

Anderson, Mark M. "Five 'Crucial Events' in the Life of W. G. Sebald." *Kosmopolis* (February 23, 2015). http://kosmopolis.cccb.org/en/sebal diana/post/cinc-esdeveniments-a-la-vida-de-w-g-sebald/

Atkin, Rhian. *Saramago's Labyrinths: A Journey through Form and Content in Blindness and All the Names*. Manchester: Manchester University Press, 2012.

Atkin, Rhian. "Tell It Again, José! Some Principles of Digression in Saramago." In *Textual Wanderings: The Theory and Practice of Narrative Digression*, edited by Rhian Atkin. London: Legendam 2011, 99–111.

Austen, Jane. *Emma* (1815), edited by Fiona Stafford. New York: Penguin Classics, 2015.

Babel, Isaac. *Collected Stories*, edited and translated by Walter Morison. New York: Criterion Books, 1955.

Baker, Nicholson. "The History of Punctuation" (1993). In *The Size of Thoughts: Essays and Other Lumber*. New York: Random House, 1996, 70–88.

Baldwin, James. *James Baldwin: Early Novels and Stories*, edited by Toni Morrison. New York: Library of America, 1998.

Baldwin, James. *James Baldwin: Later Novels*, edited by Darryl Pinckney. New York: Library of America, 2015.

Baldwin, James. *Notes of a Native Son* (1955). New York: Bantam, 1966.

Blatt, Ben. "How Many Exclamation Points Do Great Writers Use?: A Very Short Book Excerpt." *The Atlantic* (March 2017). https://ww w.theatlantic.com/magazine/archive/2017/03/curb-your-enthusi asm/513833/

BLD in MT. "William Faulkner's Fabulous Compound Words." (February 6, 2015). http://bld-in-mt.blogspot.com/2015/02/william -faulkners-fabulous-compound.html

Bleikasten, André. *Faulkner's "As I Lay Dying,"* translated by Roger Little. Bloomington: Indiana University Press, 1973.

Boone, Joseph Allen. *Libidinal Currents: Sexuality and the Shaping of Modernism.* Chicago: University of Chicago Press, 1998.

Boren, Mark Edelman. "More than a Line: The Unmistakable Impression of Significance and the Dashes of Henry James." *Philological Quarterly* 77.3 (Summer 1998): 329–47.

Bosanquet, Theodora. *Henry James at Work* (1924), edited by Lyall H. Powers. Ann Arbor: University of Michigan Press, 2006. http://sit e.ebrary.com/lib/princeton/Doc?id=10392998&ppg=54

Bowers, Fredson. "Regularization and Normalization in Modern Critical Texts." *Studies in Bibliography* 42 (1989): 79–102.

Breslin, James E. "William Carlos Williams and Charles Demuth: Cross-Fertilization in the Arts." *Journal of Modern Literature* 6.2 (April 1977): 248–63.

Brody, Jennifer DeVere. *Punctuation: Art, Politics, and Play.* Durham, NC: Duke University Press, 2008.

Brownstein, Rachel. "Rachel Brownstein on Austen's Style." In Geoff Nunberg's *Language Log* (November 29, 2010). https://languagelog. ldc.upenn.edu/nll/?p=2805

Calhoun, Adam J. "Punctuation in Novels." (February 15, 2016). https:// medium.com/@neuroecology/punctuation-in-novels-8f316d542ec4

Cameron, Sharon. *Choosing Not Choosing: Dickinson's Fascicles.* Chicago: University of Chicago Press, 1992.

Cameron, Sharon. "Dickinson's Fascicles." In *The Emily Dickinson Handbook*, edited by Gudrun Grabher, Roland Hagenbüchle, and Cristanne Miller. Amherst: University of Massachusetts Press, 1998, 138–60.

Cameron, Sharon. *Lyric Time: Dickinson and the Limits of Genre.* Baltimore: Johns Hopkins University Press, 1979.

Carey, J. V. *Punctuation.* London: Cambridge University Press, 1957.

Cather, Willa. *The Professor's House.* Vintage, 1925.

Costello, Bonnie. "William Carlos Williams in a World of Painters." Review of *A Recognizable Image. Boston Review* (June/July 1979). http://bostonreview.net/archives/BR04.6/costello.html

Crair, Ben. "The Period Is Pissed." *New Republic* (November 25, 2013). http://www.newrepublic.com/article/115726/period-our-simples t-punctuation-mark-has- become-sign-anger

Crumbley, Paul. *Inflections of the Pen: Dash and Voice in Emily Dickinson*. Lexington: University Press of Kentucky, 1996.

Cummings, E. E. [Edward Estlin]. *Complete Poems: 1904–1962*, edited by George J. Firmage. New York: Liveright, 1991.

Davidson, Jenny. *Reading Jane Austen*. New York: Cambridge University Press, 2017.

Davies, Anna. *Glyph*: A Visual Exploration of Punctuation Marks and Other Typographic Symbols*. London: Cicada Books, 2015.

de Medeiros, Paulo. "Saramago and Grass." In *In Dialogue with Saramago: Essays in Comparative Literature*, edited by Adrian Alves de Paula Martins and Mark Sabine. Manchester: Manchester Spanish and Portuguese Studies, 2006, 177–86.

Denham, Michelle. "Representations (of Time) in the Twentieth Century Novel." University of Arizona, January 2017. Abstract no: DA10110987.

Denman, Kamilla. "Emily Dickinson's Volcanic Punctuation." *The Emily Dickinson Journal* 2.1 (Spring 1993): 22–46.

Dickinson, Emily. *Emily Dickinson's Poems: As She Preserved Them*, edited by Cristanne Miller. Cambridge: Harvard University Press, 2016.

Dickinson, Emily. *The Letters of Emily Dickinson*, edited by Thomas Johnson and Theodora Ward, 3 vols. Cambridge: Harvard University Press, 1958.

Dolnick, Ben. "Semicolons: A Love Story." *The New York Times* (July 2, 2012). https://opinionator.blogs.nytimes.com/2012/07/02/semico lons-a-love-story/

Dubus, Andre. "A Love Song." In *Dancing after Hours*. New York: Alfred A. Knopf, 1996, 20–26.

Dupee, F. W. "James Baldwin and the 'Man.'" *New York Review of Books* (February 1, 1963). https://www.nybooks.com/articles/1963/02/01/j ames-baldwin-and-the-man/

Dupee, F. W. "Stevenson and the Semicolon." *EdRLS* (November 22, 2011). https://edrls.wordpress.com/2011/11/22/the-semicolon/

Dury, Richard. "Introduction." In Robert Louis Stevenson, *Strange Case of Dr. Jekyll and Mr. Hyde*, edited by Richard Dury. Edinburgh: Edinburgh University Press, 2004, xix–lxii.

Dury, Richard. "Stevenson and the Semicolon." *EdRLS* (November 22, 2011). https://edrls.wordpress.com/2011/11/22/the-semicolon/

Eliot, George. *The Mill on the Floss*, edited by Gordon S. Haight. Oxford: Oxford University Press, 2015.

Faulkner, William. *Absalom, Absalom!* (1936), New York: Vintage, 1990.

Faulkner, William. "A Rose for Emily" (1930). In *Selected Short Stories of William Faulkner*. New York: Modern Library, 1993.

Faulkner, William. *As I Lay Dying* (1930). New York: Vintage, 1990.

Faulkner, William. *Lion in the Garden: Interviews with William Faulkner*, edited by James B. Meriwether and Michael Millgate. New York: Random House, 1968.

Fisher, Laura R. "Possible Futures and Grammatical Politics in James Baldwin's *Another Country.*" *Journal of Modern Literature* 41.1 (2017): 137–55.

Fogarty, Mignon. "Dashes, Parentheses, and Commas." (May 21, 2010). http://www.quickanddirtytips.com/education/grammar/dashes-pa rentheses-and-commas?page=all

Fowler, Virginia C. *Nikki Giovanni*. New York: Twayne, 1992.

Fowler, Virginia C.. *Nikki Giovanni: A Literary Biography*. Santa Barbara, CA: Praeger, 2013.

Frederick, Samuel. "Re-reading Digression: Towards a Theory of Plotless Narrativity." In *Textual Wanderings: The Theory and Practice of Narrative Digression*, edited by Rhian Atkin. London: Legendam 2011, 15–26.

Friedman, Norman. *e. e. Cummings: The Art of His Poetry*. Baltimore: John Hopkins University Press, 1960.

Frier, David. "Righting Wrongs, Re-writing Meaning and Reclaiming the City in Saramago's *Blindness* and *All the Names.*" In *On Saramago*. Dartmouth, MA: Center for Portuguese Studies and Culture, University of Massachusetts, Dartmouth, 2001, 97–122.

Frost, Robert. *The Letters of Robert Frost. Volume 1*, 1886–1921, edited by Donald Sheehy, Mark Richardson, Robert Faggen. Cambridge: Harvard University Press, 2014.

Giltrow, Janet, and David Stouck. "Lyrical Measures: Cohesion and Sentence Endings in Cather's Prose." *Willa Cather Pioneer Memorial Newsletter* 35.3 (Fall 1991): 11–15.

Gingrich, Brian. *The Pace of Fiction: Narrative Movement and the Novel, Fielding to Joyce*. New York: Oxford University Press, 2020.

Giovanni, Nikki. *The Collected Poetry of Nikki Giovanni: 1968–1998*, edited by Virginia C. Fowler. New York: William Morrow, 2003.

Goldman, Nathan. "'The Power of W. G. Sebald's Small Silences." *Literary Hub* (May 18, 2018). https://lithub.com/the-power-of-w-g-sebalds-small-silences/

Good, Graham. "Rereading Robert Louis Stevenson." *Dalhousie Review* 62.1 (Spring 1982): 44–59.

Halter, Peter. "Williams and the Visual Arts." In *The Cambridge Companion to William Carlos Williams*, edited by Christopher MacGowan. New York: Cambridge University Press, 2016, 37–52.

Hartman, Charles O. *Verse: An Introduction to Prosody*. Chichester, West Sussex: Wiley Blackwell, 2015.

Hartman, Geoffrey H. "The Voice of the Shuttle: Language from the Point of View of Literature." In *Beyond Formalism: Literary Essays 1958–1970*. New Haven: Yale University Press, 1970, 337–55.

Hawthorne, Nathaniel. *The Scarlet Letter* (1850). Harmondsworth: Penguin, 1986.

Hemingway, Ernest. *Death in the Afternoon*. New York: Charles Scribner's Sons, 1932.

Hemingway, Ernest. "Hills Like White Elephants" (1927). In *The Oxford Book of American Short Stories*, edited by Joyce Carol Oates, 2nd ed. New York: Oxford University Press, 2013.

Hemingway, Ernest. *In Our Time* (1925). New York: Scribner's, 1996.

Hemingway, Ernest. *The Sun Also Rises* (1926). New York: Macmillan, 1986.

Henley, Jon. "The End of the Line?" *The Guardian* (April 3, 2008). https://www.theguardian.com/world/2008/apr/04/france.britishidentity

Heyen, William. "In Consideration of Cummings" (1973). In *Critical Essays on E. E. Cummings*, edited by Guy Rotella. Boston: G. K. Hall, 1984, 232–42.

Howe, Susan. *My Emily Dickinson*. Berkeley: North Atlantic Books, 1985.

Howe, Susan. *The Birth-Mark: Unsettling the Wilderness in American Literary History*. Hanover, NH: Wesleyan University Press of New England, 1993.

Hynes, Sam. "Cummings' *Collected Poems*, 276." *Explicator* 10.2 (1951): Item 9: 19.

Irving, Washington. "Rip Van Winkle." In *Washington Irving: History, Tales and Sketches*. New York: Library of America, 1983, 769–85.

Jacobs, Carol. *Sebald's Vision*. New York: Columbia University Press, 2015.

Jaggi, Maya. "Recovered Memories," interview of W. G. Sebald. In *The Guardian* (September 21, 2001). https://www.theguardian.com/books/2001/sep/22/artsandhumanities.highereducation

James, Henry. *In the Cage & Other Tales*, edited by Morton Dauwen Zabel. New York: W. W. Norton, 1969.

James, Henry. *The Ambassadors* (1903). Harmondsworth: Penguin 2008.

James, Henry. *"The Turn of the Screw" & Other Short Fiction*. New York: Bantam, 1981.

Jameson, Fredric. *Marxism and Form: Twentieth-Century Dialectical Theories of Literature*. Princeton: Princeton University Press, 1972.

Jameson, Fredric. *Sartre: The Origins of a Style* (1961). New York: Columbia University Press, 1984.

Jarosz, Anna Maria, Ben Bosse, Ben Bosse, Anna Maria Jarosz, Bruno Jeremy Flörke, Henry Chase Richards, Herle Andkjær, Jacob Mark Rørhøj, Paulina Anna Gretkierewicz and Rachel Tatum. "Unraveling Austerlitz." *Roskilde Universitetscenter's Digitale Arkiv* (Fall 2014), 96 pages. https://core.ac.uk/display/43029606/tab/similar-list

Joyce, James. *Ulysses* (1922). New York: Alfred A. Knopf, 1997.

Kennedy, Maev. "Pride, Prejudice and Poor Punctuation." *The Guardian* (October 22, 2010). https://www.theguardian.com/books/2010/oct/23/jane-austen-poor-punctuation-kathryn-sutherland

Kennedy, Richard S. *E. E. Cummings Revisited*. New York: Twayne, 1994.

Kidder, Rushworth M. *E. E. Cummings: An Introduction to the Poetry*. New York: Columbia University Press, 1979.

Kilyovski, Vakrilen. "The Nude, the Grasshopper, and the Poet-Painter: A Reading of E. E. Cummings' 'r-p-o-p-h-e-s-s-a-g-r.'" *Spring* 20 (October 2013): 99–109.

Krasznahorkai, László. *The Last Wolf*, translated by George Szirtes. New York: New Directions, 2009.

Kunsa, Ashley. "Mystery and Possibility in Cormac McCarthy." *Journal of Modern Literature* 35.2 (2012): 146–52.

Leiter, Sharon. *Critical Companion to Emily Dickinson: A Literary Reference to Her Life and Work*. New York: Facts on File, 2007.

Lennard, John. *But I Digress: The Exploitation of Parentheses in English Printed Verse*. Oxford: Clarendon Press, 1991.

Link, Alex. "Staking Everything On It: A Stylistic Analysis of Linguistic Patterns in 'Hills Like White Elephants.'" *Hemingway Review* 23.2 (Spring 2004): 66–74.

Lockwood, Preston. "'But What Are We Talking About?': Henry James's First Interview." *The New York Times* (March 21, 1915).

Long, J. J. *W. G. Sebald—Image, Archive, Modernity*. Edinburgh: Edinburgh University Press, 2007.

MacLeod, Glen. "Williams and His Contemporaries." In *The Cambridge Companion to William Carlos Williams*, edited by Christopher MacGowan. New York: Cambridge University Press, 2016, 24–36.

Malvern, Jack. "It Is a Truth Universally Acknowledged That Jane Austen Didn't Do Punctuation—Dash It." *The Australian* (August 19, 2010). https://www.theaustralian.com.au/arts/books/it-is-a-truth-un iversally-acknowledged-that- jane-austen-didnt-do-punctuation-da sh-it/news-story/2a248b9eec7fc75320f9c64509c51bba

Matore, Daniel. "Cummings's Typewriter Language: The Typography of *Tulips & Chimneys*." *Textual Practice* 31.7 (Summer 2017): 1509–31.

McCarthy, Cormac. *The Road*. New York: Alfred A. Knopf, 2006.

McCulloch, Gretchen. *Because Internet: Understanding the New Rules of Language*. New York: Riverhead Books, 2019.

McCulloh, Mark R. *Understanding W. G. Sebald*. Columbia: University of South Carolina Press, 2003.

Menand, Louis. "Bad Comma: Lynne Truss's Strange Grammar." *The New Yorker* (June 28, 2004). https://www.newyorker.com/magazine/ 2004/06/28/bad-comma

Menikoff, Barry. *Robert Louis Stevenson and "The Beach of Falesá."* Edinburgh: Edinburgh University Press, 1984.

Meyer, Charles F. *A Linguistic Study of American Punctuation*. New York: Peter Lang, 1987.

Miller, Andrew. "Zero Visibility." *The New York Times on the* Web (October 4, 1998). https://archive.nytimes.com/www.nytimes.com/b ooks/98/10/04/reviews/981004.04millert.html

Miller, Cristanne. *Emily Dickinson: A Poet's Grammar*. Cambridge: Harvard University Press, 1987.

Miller, J. Hillis. *Poets of Reality: Six Twentieth-Century Writers*. Cambridge: Harvard University Press, 1965.

Mitchell, Lee Clark. *Mere Reading: The Poetics of Wonder in Modern American Novels*. New York: Bloomsbury, 2017.

Mitchell, Lee Clark. *More Time: Late Styles and Contemporary Short Stories*. New York: Oxford University Press, 2019.

Moore, Marianne. "People Stare Carefully" (1926). In *Critical Essays on E. E. Cummings*, edited by Guy Rotella. Boston: G. K. Hall, 1984, 46–49.

Moretti, Franco. *Modern Epic*. New York: Verso, 1996.

Morrison, Toni. *Beloved* (1987). New York: Vintage, 2004.

Moss, Roger B. "Sterne's Punctuation." *Eighteenth-Century Studies* 15.2 (Winter 1981–82): 179–200.

Nabokov, Vladimir. *Lectures on Literature*, edited by Fredson Bowers. New York: Harcourt Brace Jovanovich, 1980.

Nabokov, Vladimir *The Annotated Lolita: Revised and Updated* (1955), edited by Alfred Appel, Jr. New York: Random House, Inc., 1991.

Norris, Mary. *Between You & Me: Confessions of a Comma Queen*. New York: W. W. Norton, 2015.

Nowell, Isaac. "One Sentence on Top of Another: On László Krasznahorkai's 'The Last Wolf.'" *Los Angeles Review of Books* (May 9, 2017) https://lareviewofbooks.org/article/one-sentence-on-top -of-another-on-laszlo- krasznahorkais-the-last-wolf/

Oliver, Mary. "Mary Oliver on the Magic of Punctuation" (2001). *BrainPickings* (September 10, 2014). https://www.brainpickings.org/ 2014/09/10/mary-oliver-on-punctuation/

Ong, Walter. "Historical Backgrounds of Elizabethan and Jacobean Punctuation Theory." *PMLA* 59.2 (June 1944): 349–60.

Page, Philip. *Dangerous Freedom: Fusion and Fragmentation in Toni Morrison's Novels*. Jackson: University of Mississippi Press, 1995.

Parkes, M. B. *Pause and Effects: An Introduction to the History of Punctuation in the West*. Berkeley: University of California Press, 1992.

Partridge, Eric. *You Have a Point There*. London: Hamish Hamilton, 1953.

Persson, Torleif. "Impersonal Style and the Form of Experience in W. G. Sebald's *The Rings of Saturn*." *Studies in the Novel* 28.2 (Summer 2016): 205–22.

Poe, Edgar Allen. "The Tell-Tale Heart." In *The Fall of the House of Usher and Other Writings*. Harmondsworth: Penguin, 2003, 228–33.

Proust, Marcel. "A propos du "style" de Flaubert." *Sainte-Beuve*. Paris: Gallimard/Folio, 1971, 586–600.

Provance, Phill. "What Does a Lack of Punctuation Signify in a Poem?" (November 20, 2017). https://www.quora.com/What-does-a-lack-o f-punctuation-signify-in-a-poem

Radford, Ceri. "Dash It All – Give Jane Austen the Last Word." *The Telegraph* (August 20, 2010). https://www.telegraph.co.uk/culture/ books/7955526/Dash-it-all-give-Jane-Austen-the-last-word.html.

Raine, Craig. "Afterword." In Vladimir Nabokov, *Lolita*. Harmondsworth: Penguin, 1995, 319–31.

Randel, Fred V. "Parentheses in Faulkner's *Absalom, Absalom!*" *Style* 5.1 (Winter 1971): 70–87.

Rée, Jonathan. "Funny Voices: Stories, Punctuation, and Personal History." *New Literary History* 21.4 (Autumn 1990): 1039–105.

Riehl, Robin Vella. "James and the 'No-Comma': Punctuation and Authority in 'Daisy Miller.'" *Henry James Review* 35.1 (Winter 2014): 68–75.

Sandarg, Eric. "Faulkner's Stylistic Difficulty: A Formal Analysis of *Absalom, Absalom!*" Dissertation, Georgia State University, 2017. https://scholarworks.gsu.edu/english_diss/189

Saramago, José. *Blindness* (1995), translated by Giovanni Pontiero, New York: Harcourt, 1997.

Scheible, Jeff. *Digital Shift: The Cultural Logic of Punctuation.* Minneapolis: University of Minnesota Press, 2015. https://www-jst or-org.ezproxy.princeton.edu/stable/10.5749/j.ctt13x1mbw

Sebald, W. G. *Austerlitz* (2001), translated by Anthea Bell. New York: Random House, 2001.

Sebald, W. G. *The Rings of Saturn* (1995), translated by Michael Hulse. New York: New Directions, 1995.

Smith, Marquard. "Theses on the Philosophy of History: The Word of Research in the Age of Digital Searchability and Distributability." *Journal of Visual Culture* 12.3 (December 2013): 375–403.

Stein, Gertrude. "Gertrude Stein: Poetry & Grammar." *Lemonhound 3.0.* (October 13, 2012). https://lemonhound.com/2012/10/13/gertru de-stein-poetry-grammar/

Sternlieb, Lisa. *The Female Narrator in the British Novel: Hidden Agendas.* London: Palgrave, 2002.

Stewart, Garrett. *The Value of Style in Fiction.* New York: Cambridge University Press, 2018.

Strunk, William Jr. and E. B. White. *The Elements of Style.* New York: Macmillan, 1979.

Strychacz, Thomas. "*In Our Time*, Out of Season." In *The Cambridge Companion to Ernest Hemingway*, edited by Scott Donaldson. New York: Cambridge University Press, 1996, 55–86.

Sutherland, Kathryn. "Austen's Points: Kathryn Sutherland Responds." In Geoff Nunberg's *Language Log* (November 29, 2010). https://la nguagelog.ldc.upenn.edu/nll/?p=2811

Sutherland, Kathryn. *Jane Austen's Textual Lives: From Aeschylus to Bollywood.* Oxford: Oxford University Press, 2005.

Tamplin, John. Blackboard post for ENG 357, Fall 2013.

Teall, F. Horace. *Punctuation.* New York: D. Appleton and Company, 1901.

Tolomeo, Diane. "The Final Octagon of *Ulysses.*" *James Joyce Quarterly* 10.4 (Summer 1973): 439–54.

Truss, Lynne. *Eats, Shoots and Leaves: The Zero Tolerance Approach to Punctuation*. New York: Gotham Books, 2004.

Victor, Daniel. "Oxford Comma Dispute Is Settled as Maine Drivers Get $5 Million." *The New York Times* (February 9, 2018). https://www.nytimes.com/2018/02/09/us/oxford-comma-maine.html.

Watson, Cecelia. *Semicolon: The Past, Present, and Future of a Misunderstood Mark*. New York: Ecco, 2019.

Weisbuch, Robert. *Emily Dickinson's Poetry*. Chicago: University of Chicago Press, 1975.

Weisbuch, Robert. "Prisming Dickinson; or, Gathering Paradise by Letting Go." In *The Emily Dickinson Handbook*, edited by Gudrun Grabher, Roland Hagenbüchle, and Cristanne Miller. Amherst: University of Massachusetts Press, 1998, 197–223.

White, Duncan. "'(I Have Camouflaged Everything, My Love)': *Lolita's* Pregnant Parentheses." *Nabokov Studies* 9 (2005): 47–64.

Williams, Arthur. "W. G. Sebald's Three-Letter Word: On the Parallel World of the English Translations." In *A Literature of Restitution: Critical Essays on W. G. Sebald*, edited by Jeannette Baxter, Valerie Henitiuk and Ben Hutchinson. Manchester: Manchester University Press, 2013, 25–41.

Williams, James. "Beckett between the Words: Punctuation and the Body in the English Prose." *Samuel Beckett Today / Aujourd'hui* 24 (2012): 249–58.

Williams, William Carlos. *William Carlos Williams: Selected Poems*, edited by Charles Tomlinson. New York: New Directions, 1985.

Wood, James. "Madness and Civilization: The Very Strange Fictions of László Krasznahorkai." (July 4, 2011). https://www.newyorker.com/magazine/2011/07/04/madness-and-civilization

Woolf, Virginia. *Mrs. Dalloway* (1925). New York: Harcourt Brace, 2005.

Wulfman, Clifford. "The Poetics of Ruptured Mnemosis: Telling Encounters in William Faulkner's *Absalom, Absalom!*" *The Faulkner Journal* 20.1/2 (Fall 2004): 111–32.

Wyatt, Jean. *Love and Narrative Form in Toni Morrison's Later Novels*. Athens: University of Georgia Press, 2017.

Yagoda, Ben. "Mad Dash." *The New York Times* (October 22, 2012). https://opinionator.blogs.nytimes.com/2012/10/22/mad-dash/

Index